Handmade
Fabric
Flowers

HANDMADE FABRIC FLOWERS
Copyright © 2009 Elegant Books Taiwan

Originally published in Traditional Chinese language by Elegant Books Culture Enterprise Co. Ltd Taiwan.

English language rights, translation and production by World Book Media, LLC
info@worldbookmedia.com

English technical editor: Jan Wutkowski
English editor: Lindsay Fair

Printed in China.
For information, address St. Martin's Press,
175 Fifth Avenue, New York, N.Y. 10010
www.stmartins.com

Library of Congress Cataloging-in-Publication Data Available Upon Request
ISBN 978-1-250-00902-9

First U.S. Edition: August 2012

10 9 8 7 6 5 4 3 2 1

Handmade Fabric Flowers

32 Beautiful Blooms to Make

You-Zhen Lu

St. Martin's Griffin
New York

Contents

Introduction

Although they may be small and delicate, flowers possess immense power: they influence our moods by bringing cheer and symbolize our emotions, such as love, friendship, and good will. By handcrafting flowers from fabric, it is possible to capture these sentiments forever.

Handmade Fabric Flowers introduces readers to the flower iron—a specialized tool that allows crafters to create more detailed flowers than ever before. Equipped with various interchangeable tool heads, the easy to use flower iron adds realistic shape and texture to petals, leaves, and stamens.

There are endless uses for the fabric flowers you will create: embellish any outfit with a fabric flower brooch, hat, or headband for one-of-a-kind style, add beauty and elegance to your home with an artful fabric flower arrangement, or commemorate a special event, such as a wedding, with a handcrafted bouquet or centerpiece. Some of the projects in this book are presented with specific uses in mind: follow the instructions or feel free to make modifications and create your own designs. Let the beauty of these flowers inspire you!

The Flowers

01. Dahlia

An exceptionally diverse flower, Dahlias grow in a rainbow of colors and range in size from tiny pompoms to enormous dinner plates. In this version, organza petals are twisted into shape and sprinkled with pearlescent beads to create a breathtaking bloom.

❧ Instructions on page 66

02. Balloon Flower

Named for their resemblance to hot air balloons as unopened buds, Balloon Flowers possess a truly distinctive shape. In this fabric incarnation, sheer organza is gathered to create voluminous petals and embellished with decorative pearls.

❧ Instructions on page 68

03. Penny Black

Extraordinarily rare for flowers, Penny Black naturally occurs in a shade of purple so dark that it actually appears black. With a sharply contrasting white edge and gracefully trailing shape, this flower makes a stunning brooch to complement any outfit.

❀ Instructions on page 70

04. *Shasta Daisy*

With yellow centers surrounded by snowy white petals, Shasta Daisies are similar to the common meadow daisy, but have larger, more abundant flowers. The white color scheme makes it a classic choice for weddings. Use a single bloom to accent a dress or make an entire bouquet.

❀ Instructions on page 72

05. Campanula

With a scientific name that translates to "little bell," this flower makes a charming corsage or boutonniere. Silk petals are artfully arranged into a fan to mimic the Campanula, or Bellflower's unique tubular shape.

❀ Instructions on page 75

o6. Sunflower

Symbolizing warmth and happiness, these Sunflowers make a cheerful get-well-soon gift. Thoughtful details, like beading and scalloped ribbon, combine with rich, fiery-hued fabrics to capture the majestic splendor of these summertime favorites.

❧ Instructions on page 78

07. Peony

With their lush, full blooms, Peonies symbolize prosperity and good fortune. Combine fabrics with different colors or textures to add dimension and for more impact.

❀ Instructions on page 80

o8. Geum Lady Stratheden

Known for its double flowers and long blooming season, Geum Lady Stratheden is a popular choice among summer gardeners. Mix solid and print fabrics to create a stylish accessory inspired by this "ladylike" flower.

❀ Instructions on page 83

09. Plum Blossom

As an early bloomer, the Plum Blossom appears on fruit trees in midwinter. Enjoy this beauty year-round by pinning it to your favorite shawl.

❉ Instructions on page 85

10. Japanese Anemone

Reaching heights up to five feet tall, the Japanese Anemone is a perennial favorite that blooms every fall. Composed of textured eyelet fabric and an abundance of stamens, this version of the Japanese Anemone is every bit as stately as one you'd find growing in a garden.

❀ Instructions on page 88

11. Orchid

Known as delicate, exotic creatures, Orchids are often considered the most graceful of all flowers. Craft these blossoms from satin and rhinestones and attach to a simple branch to create an elegant decoration for the home.

❁ Instructions on page 92

12. Gerber Daisy

Perfect for brightening a friend's day, the vibrant colors and large blooms of Gerber Daisies are known for bringing cheer. Bursting with texture, this flower makes a lively brooch or hair accessory.

❀ Instructions on page 95

13. Forget Me Not

Throughout history, these diminutive flowers have served as a symbol of enduring love and remembrance. With special details like beaded stamens and wired leaves, no one will overlook these sweet blooms. Add a bow to your Forget Me Not bouquet for a one-of-a-kind corsage.

❧ Instructions on page 97

14. Daisy

Drawing inspiration from childhood, this bracelet design offers a stylish and modern version of the Daisy chain. Thread flowers of organza and lace onto a simple cord for a Daisy chain that will stay fresh forever.

❧ Instructions on page 100

15. Hellebores

Sometimes referred to as a Christmas Rose, Hellebores are the blooms of the late winter garden. These small flowers are shown here as a trio made from either burlap or cotton fabric. These demure blooms are perfect as decorative embellishments to small accessories, like hair clips, or as an understated corsage.

❅ Instructions on page 102

16. Bachelor's Button

Named for its use as a boutonniere flower, a single Bachelor's Button bloom garners attention. Cutting a sawtooth edge into satin petals replicates the flower's fluffy shape. Add a pin back to turn this flower into a statement piece for your favorite jacket.

❀ Instructions on page 104

17. Double Impatiens

With an abundance of colorful petals, Double Impatiens resemble miniature roses. Made from silk, this cheerful flower makes a sweet addition to any headband.

❀ Instructions on page 106

20. Freesia

Freesia grows in clusters of upward facing, funnel-shaped flowers. Embroidered lace details add dimension, while plastic tubing provides structure. Arrange these flowers in a small vase for a realistic floral display.

❧ Instructions on page 115

21. Rosa Rugosa

Commonly called the Beach Rose, this flower may appear to be a delicate beauty, but it is actually quite hardy and flourishes carefree along the coastline. Sheer petals and pearl stamens make this graceful flower the perfect embellishment.

❉ Instructions on page 118

22. Tulip Poplar

Surprisingly, these showy flowers bloom on trees that grow to be one hundred feet tall. Realistic details, such as fringe and pearl stamens, replicate the unique structure of the Tulip Poplar.

Instructions on page 121

23. Ranunculus

With endless layers of delicate, tissue-paper thin petals, Ranunculus flowers could easily be mistaken for works of origami. In this fabric version, sheer ribbon is affixed to cotton in order to achieve that lustrous sheen distinctive to Ranunculus.

❧ Instructions on page 124

24. Anemone

Composed of linen petals and sequin stamens, this fabric Anemone, or Windflower, is just as magical as the real-life version. Throughout mythology, these flowers serve as symbols of good luck and are used to protect against evil. The simple beauty of this flower makes it ideal for a brooch.

❧ Instructions on page 126

25. Miniature Rose

The Miniature Rose's perfectly shaped tiny blooms make it one of the sweetest flowers around. Combine two shades of the same color for a traditional look, or mix a solid and a print fabric for a bit of flair.

❀ Instructions on page 128

26. Cosmos

Named for its evenly spaced petals, Cosmos means "harmony" or "balanced universe" in Greek. Attach a pair of these petite blooms to a barrette for a dainty hair accessory.

❁ Instructions on page 131

27. Carnation

Dating back to ancient times, the Carnation is one of the most popular and meaningful flowers. Due to their symbolic significance, these flowers make great gifts. Consider color when making your fabric choice, as different colors represent different messages, such as pink for gratitude and red for love.

❧ Instructions on page 133

28. Begonia

With flowers ranging from red, pink, orange, yellow, and white, plus variegated, often striped leaves, Begonias are among the most dimensional plants. Experiment with different prints and patterns to replicate the colorful nature of this flower.

❧ Instructions on page 135

29. Summer Wine Rose

It's all about the details with this flower. Combine cotton and voile fabrics and treat the petals with a special ironing technique to achieve dimension and texture. For effortless elegance, pin this beauty to your favorite bag.

❧ Instructions on page 138

30. English Rose

With an abundance of petals and a heady fragrance, English Roses are magnificent when in full bloom. Press petals between layers of cheesecloth to create this realistic wrinkled texture.

❧ Instructions on page 140

31. Impatiens

As colorful, steady bloomers, Impatiens are popular among gardeners. With heart-shaped satin petals and rhinestone and pearl embellishments, this flower makes a lady-like accessory.

❈ Instructions on page 143

32. Dianthus

With a name originating from the Greek words for "god" and "flower," Dianthus has been adored for thousands of years. In this version, a special fraying technique is used to re-create the frilled petal edges characteristic of Dianthus flowers.

❀ Instructions on page 146

How to Make the Flowers

Basic Flower Making Techniques

Selecting Your Fabric

Natural fibers work best for making fabric flowers, so look for silk, cotton, linen, wool, rayon, or blends of these fibers when making your fabric selection. Avoid using synthetic fibers, such as polyester, nylon, acetate, or blends with these fibers as synthetic fibers can melt when ironed and cannot be shaped easily. Always test your fabric by ironing a scrap to see how the material reacts to heat.

In addition to fiber content, you should also consider fabric type when selecting your fabric, as this will influence the look and feel of the finished flower. Sheer, lightweight fabrics, such as chiffon and organza, are ideal for delicate flowers like dahlias, while heavier fabrics like linen and burlap are useful for details like leaves and stems. Always consider texture when choosing your fabric as it plays an important role in the appearance of your flower.

Sizing Your Fabric

Before starting to make your flower, it is important to apply sizing to your fabric. Applying sizing to your fabric will make it easier to form your flower and will help the completed flower keep its shape. There are several different sizing options available.

One popular option is gelatin sizing, which is sold in granule form and is combined with water to create a liquid product. Allow the gelatin to dissolve overnight or for immediate use, mix the gelatin with warm water, then let cool before using on fabric in order to prevent color bleeding. For best results, follow the instructions on the package. Store any leftover liquid gelatin in the refrigerator to prevent spoilage when not in use.

You can also make your own sizing by diluting one part white PVA glue with three parts water. The resulting liquid should be the consistency of milk. Keep in mind that using thicker sizing will lead to stiffer fabrics. To make the sizing solution thinner for lighter fabrics, use more water.

To apply sizing to your fabric, dip the fabric in the sizing until it becomes saturated, wring out the excess, then hang the fabric to dry. Wringing out the excess sizing may wrinkle your fabric—you can smooth out some of the wrinkles by hand and with the flower iron, but you may choose to keep them as they mimic the natural veins of petals. If you are sizing more than one color of fabric at a time, always start with light fabrics then continue with bright and dark fabrics as the dye may bleed. Alternatively, you could create separate containers of sizing for the different color ranges.

If your fabric has a napped texture, such as velvet, sponge or paint the sizing on the wrong side of the fabric and let dry.

Cutting Your Fabric

Templates are included for most of the projects in this book. Trace the templates and make a cardboard pattern. Clip or pin the pattern to your fabric and cut out around the pattern.

Follow the cutting diagram and instructions provided for each flower. The cutting diagrams are designed so that the flower pieces are cut out on the bias, or the diagonal grain of the fabric. If the flower pieces are not cut out on the bias, they will not shape properly and will fray more easily.

Applying Glue

Using the correct glue will contribute to the successful construction and neat appearance of your flowers. Flowers are almost always assembled with quick-dry tacky glue, which holds the petals together as you work.

When assembling a flower, use a small paintbrush to apply glue to the petals. The paintbrush will allow greater control and will prevent the glue from becoming visible on the finished flower. Apply glue to just a few petals at a time since the glue dries quickly. Keep in mind that the amount of glue used will have an effect on the flower's finished look: using too little glue may cause the petals to droop, while using too much glue may make the petals rigid. When applying glue, consider the shape and style of the flower and follow the instructions for each project.

Some flowers are assembled by attaching petals in rounds from the inside towards the outside. For these flowers, you may find it easier to work with the flower upside down, which will keep the petals intact while they dry and allow you to build the flower more easily.

1. Hot glue gun: Use a hot glue gun to attach your flowers to pins, barrettes, and headbands.

2. Quick-dry tacky glue: Use this fast drying glue to assemble your flowers.

3. Clear glue: Use clear glue if the area you are gluing will be visible on the completed flower.

Tools and Materials

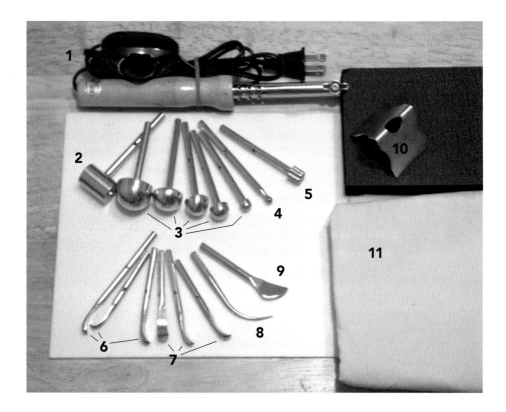

1. Flower Iron: The majority of flower irons on the market include a 60 watt 110 volt handle and a dial-operated temperature controller. If your flower iron doesn't come with a temperature controller, you should purchase one separately, for improved safety and better results.

If you are using a brand new flower iron, there a few things to keep it mind. Initially, your flower iron may smoke slightly the first time it is turned on as there may be traces of manufacturing oil present that will burn off when heated. Also, it is normal for the flower iron and tool heads to change color once they have been heated.

For best results, use the flower iron to firmly press the fabric. Pressure must be applied to add shape, even when working with light fabrics. For heavier fabrics, use more pressure and consider using a spray bottle to moisten the fabric if needed. Spray the fabric lightly, being careful not to oversaturate the fabric before ironing. This technique is also useful for fabrics that burn easily.

Flower Iron Tool Heads: There are various attachable tool heads available to add shape and texture to your fabric flowers.

2. Hammer tool head: Used to make fabric tubes for stolons (long stems).

3. Radius (30 mm, 24 mm, 21 mm, 16 mm, 10 mm) tool heads: Used to make concave petals. Larger tool heads will create wide, shallow hollows, while smaller tool heads will create narrow, deep hollows.

4. Orchid tool head: Used to shape small details of petals and leaves.

5. Forget-me-not tool head: Used to make small crimped and fluted details.

6. Chrysanthemum (1, 2, and 3-groove) tool heads: Used to make ridges and grooves, such as leaf veins.

7. Spoon (small, medium, and large) tool heads: Used to make concave hollows that are narrower than those made by the radius tool head. Larger tool heads will create wider, shallower hollows than smaller tool heads.

8. Rat tail tool head: Used to shape the edges of petals.

9. Knife tool head: Used to score details and create very deep grooves.

10. Flower Iron Rest: Always set the flower iron in the rest when not in use.

11. Ironing Pad: Use an ironing board or create an ironing pad by covering a piece of foam core with cotton. Covering the foam core with cotton will extend the life of the ironing pad. Do not cover the ironing pad with fabric that contains synthetic fibers, such as polyester, as this will melt. Alternatively, you can use a small sandbag as an ironing surface for shaping the flowers. Use natural fabric to cover the sandbag and make sure not to overstuff it, as the bag will need some give to help shape the flower.

Using the Flower Iron

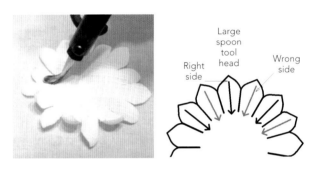

For this flower, the large spoon tool head is used to iron the petals on both sides of the fabric. This technique creates a mix of both concave and convex petals.

Safety Tips

- Secure the iron tool heads with a screwdriver before you plug in the power. Do not overtighten the screw as the metal will expand slightly when heated. When changing the tool head, it is easier and safer to let the flower iron cool slightly.
- Test the temperature of the iron with a damp cotton towel. If the water sizzles, the iron is ready.
- Use potholders or oven mitts to remove the tool heads. Place the hot tool heads on a padded surface in order to avoid leaving burn marks on tables and countertops.
- Remember that the entire flower iron shaft will be hot, not just the tool head.

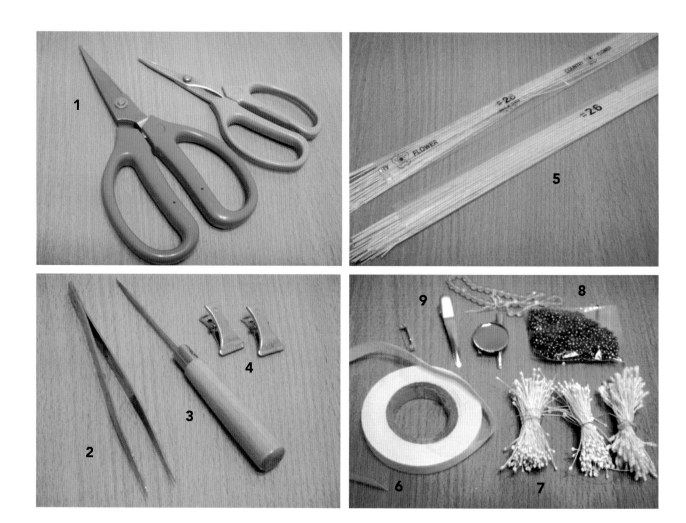

1. Scissors: To keep the blades sharp, dedicate one pair of scissors to cutting fabric and use another pair to cut anything else.

2. Tweezers: Use tweezers when working with delicate flower components, such as stamens.

3. Awl: Use the awl to punch holes in the fabric.

4. Clips: Clip the pattern to your fabric when cutting to prevent any shifting.

5. Wire: Most of the projects in this book use floral stem wire, which is usually #26 or #28 gauge, covered in white or green paper, and sold in precut lengths of about 18". Some of the projects also use beading wire, which is usually #32 or #34 gauge, bare, and sold in spools. When selecting your wire, remember the higher the gauge number, the thinner the wire.

6. Floral tape: Available in green, white, and brown and used to wrap stems.

7. Stamens: Bunches of small, pre-made stamens are used in many projects.

8. Beads: Make your own stamens using beads.

9. Pinbacks and clips: Attach pins and clips to your completed flowers to make them into wearable accessories.

Techniques

Securing the stamens:

Materials: One bunch of stamens and a 7" (18 cm)-long floral stem wire.

1. Fold the stamens in half.

2. Wrap the wire around the stamens. Twist the wire to secure.

3. Trim the stamen ends, leaving about ⅛"-⅜" (0.5-1 cm).

4. Wrap the stamen ends and wire with floral tape.

5. The stamen is complete.

Making a bow:

Materials: About 24" (60 cm) of ribbon and a 7" (18 cm)-long floral stem wire.

1. Make two loops and glue to secure.

2. Using the long ends, make two more loops and glue to secure.

3. Wrap wire around the center of the bow to secure.

01. Dahlia

❀ Shown on page 8
❀ No templates for this project

MATERIALS

7 ¾" × 8 ¾" (20 × 22 cm) sheer fabric, such as chiffon or organza

5 crystal stamens

Eight 3 mm green beads

Seven 3 mm white beads

14 ¼" (36 cm) of 5 mm fishing line

Eight 3 ½" (9 cm)-long floral stem wires

Floral tape

TOOLS

Sewing thread

Quick-dry tacky glue

Cut the fabric.

Divide the 7 ¾" × 8 ¾" (20 × 22 cm) sheer fabric into pieces according to the measurements below, then cut petals from each piece, according to the cutting diagrams below:

4 ¾" × 8 ¾" (12 × 22 cm) piece for the large rectangles
3" × 4" (8 × 10 cm) piece for the medium rectangles
2" × 4" (5 × 10 cm) piece for the small rectangles
¾" (2 cm)-wide length of sheer sparkle fabric for stem

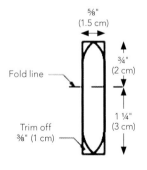

7 ¾" (20 cm)

8 ¾" (22 cm)

CUTTING DIAGRAMS FOR PETALS:

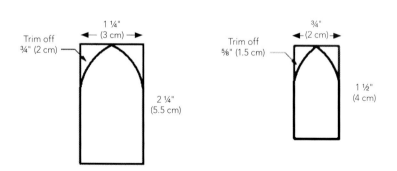

1 ¼" (3 cm)
Trim off ¾" (2 cm)
2 ¼" (5.5 cm)

From the 4 ¾" × 8 ¾" (12 × 22 cm) piece, cut sixteen large rectangles: 1 ¼" × 2 ¼" (3 × 5.5 cm) each

¾" (2 cm)
Trim off ⅝" (1.5 cm)
1 ½" (4 cm)

From the 3" × 4" (8 × 10 cm) piece, cut ten medium rectangles: ¾" × 1 ½" (2 × 4 cm) each

⅝" (1.5 cm)
Fold line
Trim off ⅜" (1 cm)
¾" (2 cm)
1 ¼" (3 cm)

From the 2" × 4" (5 × 10 cm) piece, cut ten small rectangles: ⅝" × 2" (1.5 × 5 cm) each

Make the petals.

Lay out sets of petals, each with a top and a bottom piece. Apply glue and adhere corresponding petals, for a total of 18 petal sets. Twist each petal tightly, then unfold. For the medium and large petals, wrap sewing thread about ⅛" (0.5 cm) from the base of the petals to secure.

Make the stamens.

Fold a stamen in half and attach to a floral stem wire. Wrap floral tape about ¾"-1 ¼" (2-3 cm) down the length of the wire. Make five stamens. Cut the fishing line into three equal pieces. String five beads of alternating color onto each fishing line piece and glue to secure. Fold fishing line pieces in half and attach to the remaining floral stem wires. Wrap floral tape about ¾"-1 ¼" (2-3 cm) down the length of the wire at the joint.

3 ½" (9 cm)-long floral stem wire

Assemble the flower.

1. Fold the small petals ¾" (2 cm) from the top, as shown in the cutting diagram. Apply glue to the base of each folded petal and wrap around a stamen wire.

2. Glue a medium petal to each small petal at the base. Then, glue a large petal to each medium petal for a total of five units with a small, medium, and large petal.

3. Apply glue to the base of the remaining three large petal sets and adhere to the beaded units. Arrange all the petal units in a circle. Trim excess wire, leaving a 2" (5 cm) end. Wrap and glue stem fabric around the wire.

Glue

04. *Shasta Daisy*

❀ Shown on page 12
❀ Templates on page 149

MATERIALS

6 ¼" × 6 ¾" (16 × 17 cm) velvet fabric

6 ¼" × 6 ¾" (16 × 17 cm) cotton fabric (same color as velvet)

22 small glass beads

17 mm metal honeycomb beading piece

19 ¾" (50 cm) of wide lace or ribbon

TOOLS

Quick-dry tacky glue

Beading needle

Invisible thread

Hot glue gun

Cut the fabric.

Apply tacky glue to the wrong side of the cotton fabric. Adhere the velvet fabric to cotton fabric with wrong sides together. Allow to dry to dampness—do not dry completely. Trace and cut out the small, medium, and large petal templates on page 149.

CUT OUT THE FOLLOWING PIECES:

1 small petal of damp double fabric

1 medium petal of damp double fabric

2 large petals of damp double fabric

1" × 1" (2.5 × 2.5 cm) piece of damp double fabric for calyx

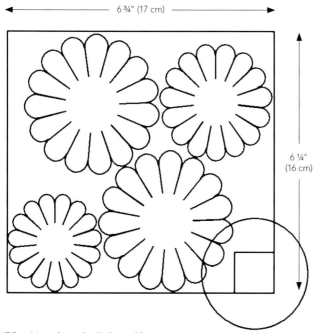

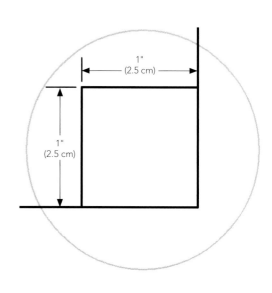

Make the petals.

While the fabric is still damp, twist the individual petal segments. Allow to dry.

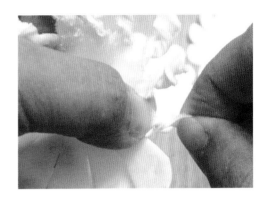

Make the stamens.

1. Trim the 1" × 1" (2.5 × 2.5 cm) piece into a circle. Glue the honeycomb piece to the velvet side of the circle using tacky glue. Cut slashes into the fabric up to the edge of the honeycomb piece.

2. Sew the beads onto the honeycomb piece.

3. Fold the slashed pieces to the back and glue in place to cover the bead stitching.

Assemble the flower.

1. Apply tacky glue to the center of each petal. Assemble the petals from smallest to largest, with the beaded honeycomb piece in the center of the smallest petal and the velvet sides facing up.

2. Fold the lace or ribbon into a bow. Pinch the bow at the center and stitch through the layers a few times to secure. Attach the flower to the bow using a hot glue gun.

05. Campanula

❀ Shown on page 14
❀ Templates on page 150

MATERIALS

3 ¼" × 8" (8.5 × 20 cm) white lining fabric, such as silk

4 ½" × 8" (11.5 × 20 cm) green or brown lining fabric, such as silk

Two beaded stamens

Twelve small stamens

Eight 7" (18 cm)-long floral stem wires

71" (180 cm) of ⅝" (1.5 cm)-wide satin ribbon

TOOLS

Quick-dry tacky glue

Hot glue gun

Cut the fabric.

Trace and cut out the ridged petal and leaf templates on page 150.

CUT OUT THE FOLLOWING PIECES:

10 ridged petal pieces of white lining fabric

10 leaves of green or brown lining fabric

1 ⅜" × 1 ½" (3.5 × 4 cm) piece of green or brown fabric for calyx

⅕" (0.5 cm)-wide lengths of green or brown fabric for stems

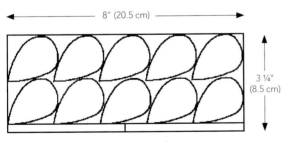

← 8" (20.5 cm) →

3 ¼" (8.5 cm)

Green or Brown Lining Fabric

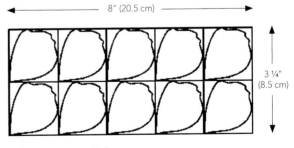

← 8" (20.5 cm) →

3 ¼" (8.5 cm)

White Lining Fabric

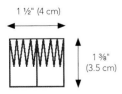

← 1 ½" (4 cm) →

1 ⅜" (3.5 cm)

Green or Brown Lining Fabric

Make the stamens.

Assemble one beaded stamen and six small stamens onto a floral stem wire. Wrap the stem fabric about 1 ¼" (3 cm) down the length of the wire. Repeat this step with the remaining stamens.

Make the calyx.

Cut a sawtooth edge into the calyx. Cut the calyx in half and curl the calyx teeth using a sharp pair of scissors.

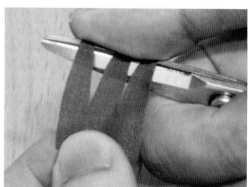

Make the petals.

1. Twist each petal tightly, then unfold.

2. Apply tacky glue to the base of five petals and overlap each by one-third to form a fan-shaped set of petals. Repeat this step for second fan-shaped set of petals.

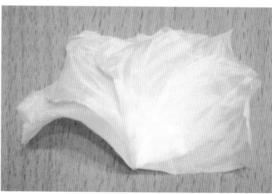

Make the leaves.

1. Lay out five sets of leaves, each with a top and bottom piece. Apply tacky glue to the center of each bottom piece. Press a wire into the glue, then add each top leaf, making sure the glue adheres to both leaf pieces in the set. Make five sets.

2. After the glue has dried, twist each leaf tightly, then unfold. Wrap and glue the ⅛" (0.5 cm)-wide stem fabric about 2" (5 cm) down the length of each wire.

Assemble the flower.

1. Apply tacky glue to the base of one fan-shaped set of petals and wrap around the stamen. Attach the calyx to the back of the assembled flower. Repeat this step for the second flower.

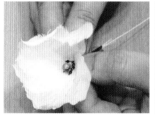

2. Arrange the two flowers and all of the leaves. Twist the wires from each piece together to secure. Cover any visible wire with stem fabric.

3. Cut the ribbon into two 35 ½" (90 cm) lengths. Tie the ribbons into a bow, as shown on page 65.

4. Attach the flowers to the bow using a hot glue gun.

o6. Sunflower

❀ Shown on page 16
❀ Templates on page 150

MATERIALS

3" × 6 ¼" (8 × 16 cm) heavy cotton slub fabric

11 ¾" (30 cm) of 1 ½" (4 cm)-wide scalloped chiffon ribbon

140 short tubular beads

24 round beads

TOOLS

Flower iron

Large spoon tool head

Beading needle

Invisible thread

Cut the fabric.

Trace and cut out the petal template on page 150.

CUT OUT THE FOLLOWING PIECES:

2 petals of heavy cotton slub fabric*

*Make sure to cut along all lines to create individual petal segments.

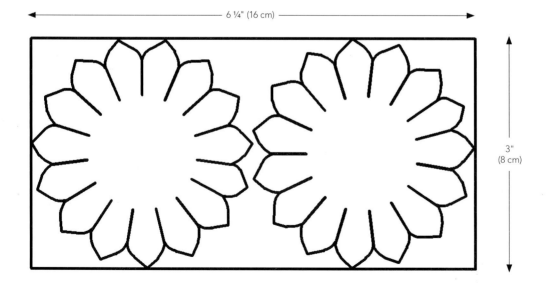

Make the stamens.

1. Using a beading needle and invisible thread, sew the beads onto one edge of the ribbon, attaching four tubular beads at a time before stitching back through the ribbon to anchor the beads. Attach a round bead within the center of each loop.

2. With a long thread, sew a running stitch ⅝" (1.5 cm) from the unbeaded edge across the entire length of the ribbon. Do not tie off the thread. Pull on the thread to gather the ribbon into a circle. Note that the outer beaded edge will be longer than the inner unbeaded edge of the ribbon.

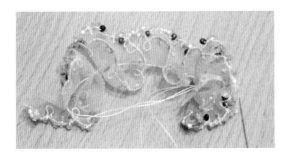

1" (2.5 cm)

Running stitch line

⅝" (1.5 cm)

Make the petals.

Using the large spoon tool head, iron each individual petal segment, as shown in the diagram. Note that every other individual petal is ironed on the wrong side. Iron both petals. Use a tacking stitch to sew the two petals together in the center.

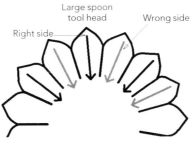

Large spoon
tool head

Wrong side

Right side

Assemble the flower.

Sew the ribbon stamen piece onto the petals.

07. Peony

❆ Shown on page 18
❆ Templates on page 150

MATERIALS

6 ⅕" × 8" (15.5 × 20.5 cm) shiny satin fabric

7 ¾" × 8" (19.5 × 20.5 cm) cotton basket weave fabric

Three 4 ¾" (12 cm)-long floral stem wires

Floral tape

TOOLS

Flower iron

Small spoon tool head

Quick-dry tacky glue

....

Cut the fabric.

Trace and cut out the calyx, small, medium, and large petal templates on page 150.

CUT OUT THE FOLLOWING PIECES:

1 calyx of basket weave fabric

10 small petals of basket weave fabric

10 medium petals of basket weave fabric

10 large petals of basket weave fabric

10 medium petals of satin fabric

10 large petals of satin fabric

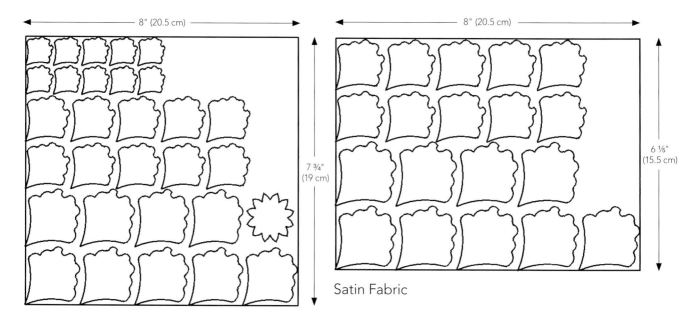

Basket Weave Fabric

Satin Fabric

Make the calyx.

Using the small spoon tool head, iron the calyx on the wrong side, as shown in the diagram. Cut a cross in the center of the calyx.

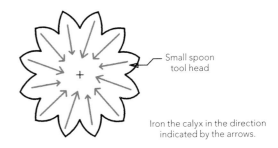

Small spoon tool head

Iron the calyx in the direction indicated by the arrows.

Make the petals.

1. Twist each petal tightly, then unfold and adjust the shape.

 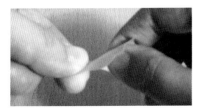  

2. Using the small spoon tool head, iron the edges of each petal, as shown in the diagram.

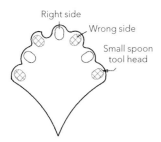  

Right side

Wrong side

Small spoon tool head

3. Apply glue to the base of each medium basket weave petal. Place a medium satin petal on top of each medium basket weave petal, leaving a ⅕" (0.5 cm) overlap. Repeat this step for the large petals.

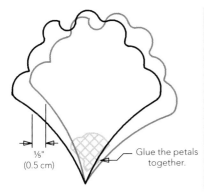 

⅕"
(0.5 cm)

Glue the petals together.

Assemble the flower.

1. Holding all three of the 4 ¾" (12 cm)-long floral stem wires as one unit, bend one end into a loop. Glue one small petal around the looped section of the wire to make the first row. Successive rows of petals will be glued into a spiral around the previous row.

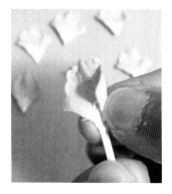

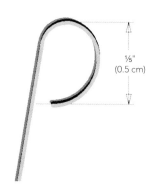

1/8"
(0.5 cm)

2. Continue spiraling the petals around the outside of the previous row to assemble the flower. Use two small petals each for the second and third rows. Use five small petals for the fourth row. Use five medium petals each for the fifth and sixth rows. Use five large petals each for the seventh and eighth rows. Make sure to overlap the petals as you glue and attach the successive outside rows.

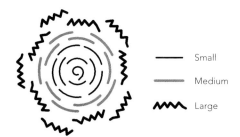

—— Small

—— Medium

∿∿ Large

3. Insert the stem wire through the calyx and glue the calyx to the back of the assembled flower. Wrap floral tape around the wire, starting at the base of the calyx and continuing ¾"-1 ¼" (2-3 cm) along the length of the wire.

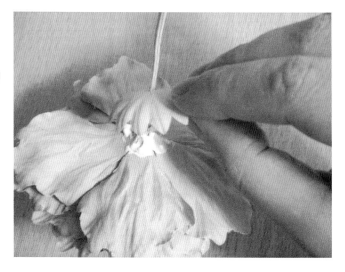

08. Geum Lady Stratheden

❧ Shown on page 20
❧ Templates on page 150

MATERIALS

4 ¼" × 5" (10.5 × 12.5 cm) cotton slub fabric

5" × 6" (12.5 × 15 cm) printed cotton/linen blend fabric

30 crystal stamens

One 3 ½" (9 cm)-long floral stem wire

TOOLS

Flower iron

3-groove chrysanthemum tool head

Quick-dry tacky glue

Cut the fabric.

Trace and cut out the calyx, small, medium, and large petal templates on page 150.

CUT OUT THE FOLLOWING PIECES:

4 small petals of cotton slub fabric

3 medium petals of cotton slub fabric

2 large petals of cotton slub fabric

1 calyx of cotton/linen blend fabric

4 small petals of cotton/linen blend fabric

3 medium petals of cotton/linen blend fabric

3 large petals of cotton/linen blend fabric

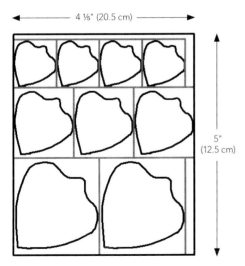

Cotton Slub Fabric

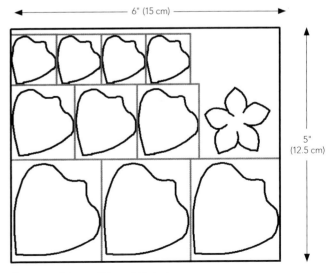

Cotton/Linen Blend Fabric

Make the petals.

1. Using the large spoon tool head, iron the petals, as shown in the diagram.

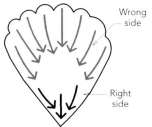

Wrong side
Right side

2. Apply glue to the base of one petal. Place a second petal on top, leaving a ¾" (2 cm) overlap. Make five sets.

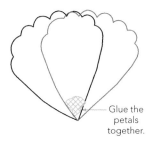

Glue the petals together.

Make the leaves.

1. Cut the suede cord into three pieces of different lengths.

2. Apply glue to the wrong side of a leaf. Attach a suede cord. Place another leaf on top, with right side facing up. Make three sets. Allow to dry.

3. Using the large spoon tool head, iron the leaf sets, as shown in the diagram.

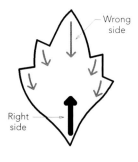

Wrong side
Right side

4. Hold the three suede cords together. Wrap with a floral stem wire and twist to secure, about ⅕" (0.5 cm) from the end.

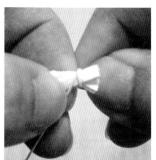

Make the stamen.

1. Insert a floral stem wire through the polystyrene ball, bend the wire, and twist to secure.

2. Apply glue to the wrong side of the 1 ¾" × 1 ¾" (3.5 × 3.5 cm) piece of cotton fabric. Cover the polystyrene ball with the fabric and trim any excess.

3. Holding all of the crystal stamens, wrap the remaining floral stem wire around the middle. Apply glue at the wire twist.

4. Insert the covered polystyrene ball wire through the center of the stamens.

Assemble the flower.

1. Apply glue to the base of each petal. Attach the petals to the stamen. Make sure to spiral and overlap the petals when gluing.

2. Cut a slit in the center of the calyx. Insert the stamen wire through the calyx and glue the calyx to the back of the assembled flower. Glue the leaves to the back of the assembled flower. Trim the wires to 2"-2 ¾" (5-6 cm). Wrap the stem fabric around the wire and secure with glue.

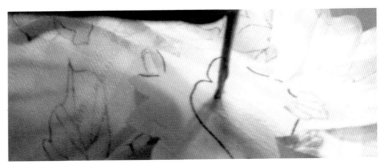

10. Japanese Anemone

❁ Shown on page 24
❁ Templates on page 151

MATERIALS

6 ⅛" × 6 ⅛" (15.5 × 15.5 cm) cotton eyelet fabric

4 ¼" × 4 ½" (11 × 11.5 cm) cotton slub fabric

120 rose stamens

Five 7" (18 cm)-long floral stem wires

TOOLS

Flower iron

Large spoon tool head

Quick-dry tacky glue

Cut the fabric.

Trace and cut out the petal and leaf templates on page 151.

CUT OUT THE FOLLOWING PIECES:

4 petals of cotton eyelet fabric

6 leaves of cotton slub fabric

Two 1" × 1 ¼" (2.5 × 3 cm) pieces of cotton slub fabric for the calyxes

Five ⅕" × 2 ½" (0.5 × 6 cm) pieces of cotton slub fabric for the stems

⅜" × 4 ¼" (1 × 11 cm) piece of cotton slub fabric for the stems

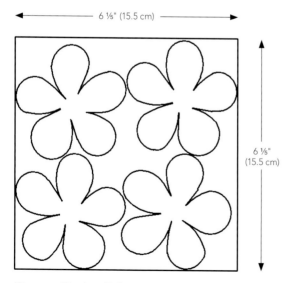

Cotton Eyelet Fabric

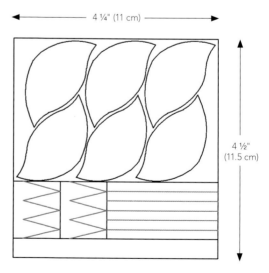

Cotton Slub Fabric

Make the petals.

Using the large spoon tool head, iron the petals, as shown in the diagram.

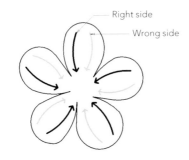

Make the calyx.

Cut a sawtooth edge into the calyx pieces. Curl the calyx teeth using a sharp pair of scissors.

Make the leaves.

1. Lay out three sets of leaves, each with a top and bottom piece. Apply glue to the center of each bottom piece. Press a floral stem wire into the glue, leaving a ⅕" (0.5 cm) space at the top of each leaf. Add each top leaf, making sure the glue adheres to both leaf pieces in the set. Make three sets.

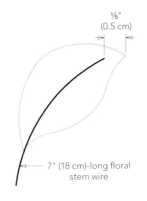

2. Using the large spoon tool head, iron leaves on the wrong side, as shown in the diagram.

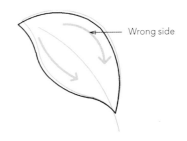

Make the stamens.

Divide the stamens into two groups: one group of 80 and one group of 40. Following the instructions on page 65, secure the stamen groups with wire. When completed, stamens should be ⅝" (1.5 cm) in length.

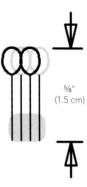

⅝"
(1.5 cm)

Assemble the flower.

1. Cut a cross and apply glue in the center of each petal. Insert one stamen group through a petal, secure, then insert through another petal. Repeat with remaining two petals and stamen group.

2. Apply glue to the uncut edge of each calyx and wrap the calyxes around the base of each flower.

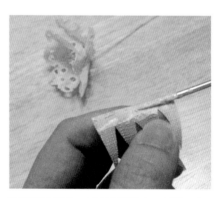

3. Wrap and glue the ⅕" (0.5 cm)-wide stem fabric around each wire, starting at the base of the flower or leaf and wrapping about ¾"-1 ¼" (2-3 cm) down the length of the wire.

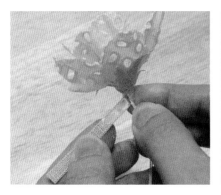

4. Arrange the flowers and leaves. Trim excess wire, leaving about 2"-2 ¼" (5-6 cm). Wrap and glue the ⅜" (1 cm)-wide stem fabric down the length of the wire.

II. Orchid

MATERIALS

5 ¾" × 7" (14.5 × 17.5 cm) shiny satin fabric

Six 4 mm rhinestone chatons

One 11 ¾" (30 cm)-long beading wire

Three 4 ¾" (12 cm)-long floral stem wires

TOOLS

Flower iron

Small spoon tool head

Quick-dry tacky glue

❀ Shown on page 26
❀ Templates on page 151

Cut the fabric.

Trace and cut out the calyx, pointed petal, and round petal templates on page 151.

CUT OUT THE FOLLOWING PIECES:

2 calyxes of satin fabric

Two 1 ½" × 4 ¾" (4 × 12 cm) pieces of satin fabric for petals

⅜" (1 cm)-wide length of satin fabric for stem

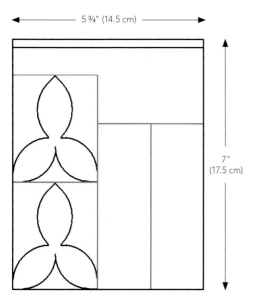

5 ¾" (14.5 cm)

7" (17.5 cm)

Make the petals.

1. Fold one of the 1 ½" × 4 ¾" (4 × 12 cm) pieces of satin into thirds and crease, as shown in the diagram below. Apply glue to the wrong side of the fabric and attach three floral stem wires. Place the second piece of satin on top with right side facing up. Allow to dry. Cut on fold lines for a total of three wired pieces.

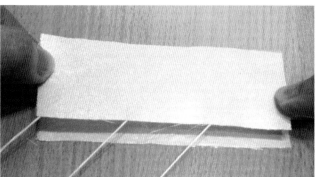

2. Using the templates, trim the wired pieces to create two pointed petals and one round petal.

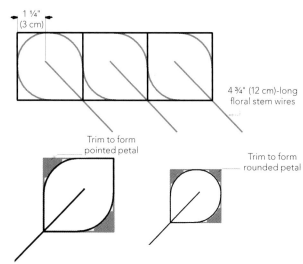

1 ¼" (3 cm)

4 ¾" (12 cm)-long floral stem wires

Trim to form pointed petal

Trim to form rounded petal

3. Using the small spoon tool head, iron the pointed and round petals, as shown in the diagram.

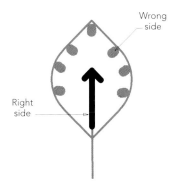

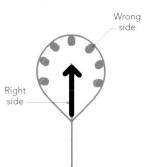

Wrong side

Right side

Wrong side

Right side

Make the calyx.

Glue the two calyx pieces with wrong sides together. Cut a cross in the center of the calyx. Using the small spoon tool head, iron the calyx on the wrong side, as shown in the diagram.

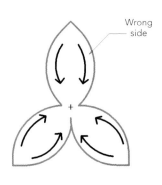

Wrong side

Make the stamen.

Thread the rhinestone chatons onto the beading wire and twist to secure.

Assemble the flower.

Arrange the petals around the rhinestone stamen. Insert the wires through the calyx with right side facing up, then glue to secure. Wrap the stem fabric around the wires and secure with glue. Adjust the petals.

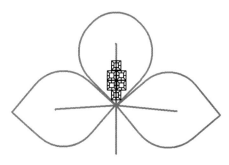

12. Gerber Daisy

❀ Shown on page 28
❀ Templates on page 152

MATERIALS

2 ¾" × 5 ½" (7 × 14 cm) faux leather

2 ¾" × 5 ½" (7 × 14 cm) cotton fabric

1 ¾" × 3 ½" (4.5 × 9 cm) cotton slub fabric

30 crystal stamens

23 ¾" (60 cm)-long pearl trim

3 ½" (9 cm)-long floral stem wire

TOOLS

Flower iron

Small spoon tool head

Quick-dry tacky glue

Hot glue gun

Cut the fabric.

Apply tacky glue to the wrong side of the faux leather. Adhere the cotton fabric with wrong sides together. Allow to dry. Trace and cut out the small and large petal templates on page 152.

CUT OUT THE FOLLOWING PIECES:

2 large petals of double fabric*

2 small petals of cotton slub fabric*

*Make sure to cut along all lines to create individual petals.

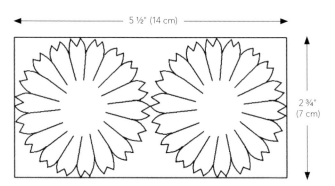

Double Fabric

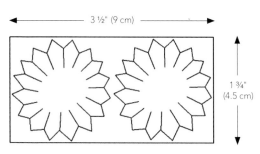

Cotton Slub Fabric

Make the petals.

Using the small spoon tool head, iron the small and large petals on the wrong side, as shown in the diagram. Cut a cross in the center of each petal.

Make the stamens.

Following the instructions on page 65, secure 30 stamens with floral stem wire. When completed, stamens should be ¾" (2 cm) in length.

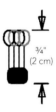

Assemble the flower.

Insert the stamen wire through the center of the two small petals, then the two large petals. Attach the pearl trim to the flower using a hot glue gun.

13. Forget Me Not

❉ Shown on page 29
❉ Template on page 152

MATERIALS

3" × 4" (7.5 × 10 cm) pink cotton slub fabric

2" × 4" (5 × 10 cm) green cotton slub fabric

10 glass beads

10 2.5 mm in diameter sequins

60" (150 cm) of beading wire

Five 4 ¾" (12 cm)-long floral stem wires

One 7" (18 cm)-long floral stem wire

23 ¾" (60 cm) of lace or lacy ribbon

Floral tape

TOOLS

Flower iron

Small spoon tool head

1-groove chrysan-themum tool head

Quick-dry tacky glue

Awl

Cut the fabric.

Trace and cut out the flower template on page 152.

CUT OUT THE FOLLOWING PIECES:

10 flowers of pink cotton slub fabric

Three ⅕" (0.5 cm)-wide lengths of pink cotton slub fabric for stems

Two ⅜" (1 cm)-wide lengths of pink cotton slub fabric for stems

Two 2" × 2" (5 × 5 cm) pieces of green cotton slub fabric for leaves

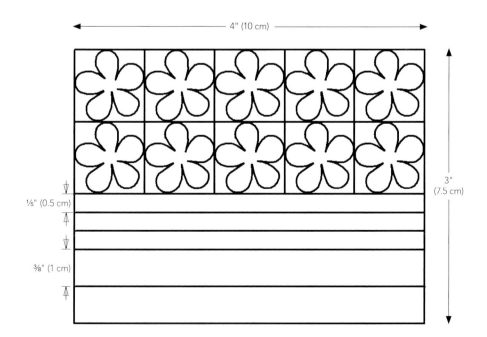

Make the flowers.

1. Using the small spoon tool head, iron the flowers on the wrong side, as shown in the diagram. Using an awl, puncture a hole in the center of each flower.

2. Insert a 6" (15 cm)-long piece of beading wire through the center of a bead, sequin, then a flower. Glue to secure. Wrap floral tape around the wire, about 1 ¼"-1 ½" (3-4 cm) down the length of the wire. Repeat for each flower.

Small spoon tool head

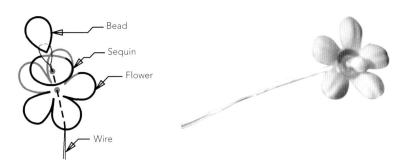

Bead

Sequin

Flower

Wire

Make the leaves.

1. Fold one piece of 2" × 2" (5 × 5 cm) green cotton slub fabric into fifths and crease, as shown in the diagram. Apply glue to the wrong side of the fabric and attach five floral stem wires to the center of each leaf, leaving a ⅛" (0.5 cm) space at the top of each leaf. Apply glue to the wrong side of the other piece of 2" × 2" (5 × 5 cm) green cotton slub fabric and place on top with right side facing up. Allow to dry.

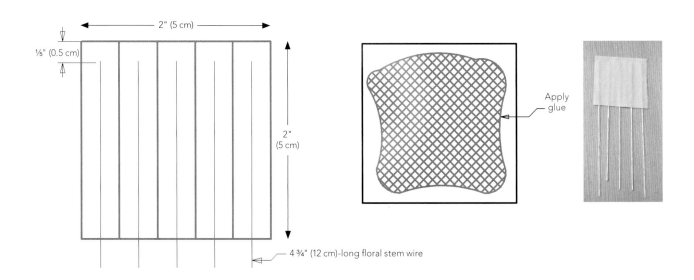

2" (5 cm)

⅛" (0.5 cm)

2" (5 cm)

Apply glue

4 ¾" (12 cm)-long floral stem wire

2. Cut on the fold lines for a total of five wired pieces. Trim each end into points. Using the 1-groove chrysanthemum tool head, iron the leaves on the wrong side, as shown in the diagram.

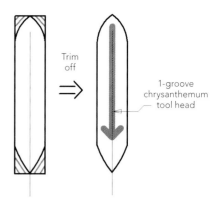

Trim off

1-groove chrysanthemum tool head

Assemble the flower.

1. Divide the 10 flowers and 5 leaves into three units. Wrap and glue the ⅛" (0.5 cm)-wide stem fabric about 1 ¼"-1 ½" (3-4 cm) down the length of each unit.

2. Tie the lace or lacy ribbon into a bow, as shown on page 65.

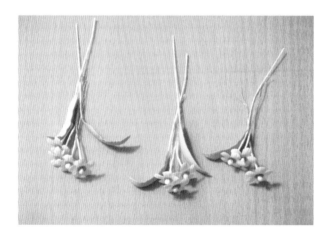

3. Arrange all three flower units. Attach the bow. Wrap and glue the ⅜" (1 cm)-wide stem fabric around the group of three stem wires.

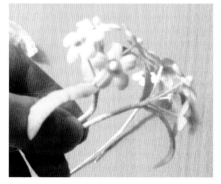

14. Daisy

❀ Shown on page 30
❀ Templates on page 152

MATERIALS

2 ¾" × 2 ¾" (7 × 7 cm) lace or embroidered fabric

2" × 2" (5 × 5 cm) embroidered or sparkle organza fabric

4 small flower-shaped beads

12 ¾" (32 cm)-long clear plastic cord

One lobster claw clasp

TOOLS

Flower iron

Rat tail tool head

Clear glue

Needle nose pliers

Cut the fabric.

Trace and cut out the small and large petal templates on page 152.

CUT OUT THE FOLLOWING PIECES:

4 large petals of lace or embroidered fabric

4 small petals of embroidered or sparkle organza fabric

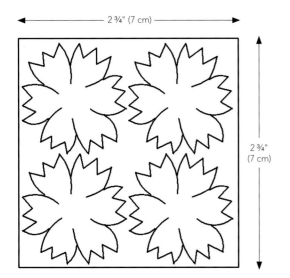

Lace or Embroidered Fabric

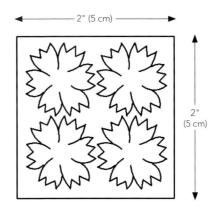

Embroidered or Sparkle
Organza Fabric

Make the petals.

Using the rat tail tool head, iron the small and large petals, as shown in the diagram. Cut a cross in the center of each petal.

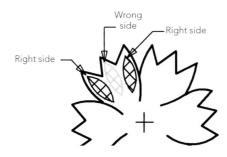

Assemble the flower.

1. Divide the cord in two. Insert one cord through the center of a large petal, a small petal, then a flower-shaped bead. The top photo shows the front view and the bottom photo shows the back view of the flower. Repeat process to string another flower onto the cord. Follow the same process to string two flowers onto the other cord.

2. Attach one end of each cord to the lobster claw using clear glue. Crimp with needle nose pliers to secure. Attach the other end of each cord to the other end of the clasp and secure.

15. *Helleborus*

❄ Shown on page 32
❄ Template on page 152

MATERIALS

4 ¼" × 7 ½" (11 × 19 cm) burlap or cotton print fabric

120 polystyrene bead stamens

Six 7" (18 cm)-long floral stem wires

1 pair of 1 ½" (40 mm) in diameter hoop earring findings

Floral tape

TOOLS

Flower iron

2-groove chrysanthemum tool head

Quick-dry tacky glue

Cut the fabric.

Trace and cut out the petal template on page 152.

CUT OUT THE FOLLOWING PIECES:

6 petals of burlap or cotton print fabric

⅜" (1 cm)-wide lengths of burlap or cotton print fabric for stems

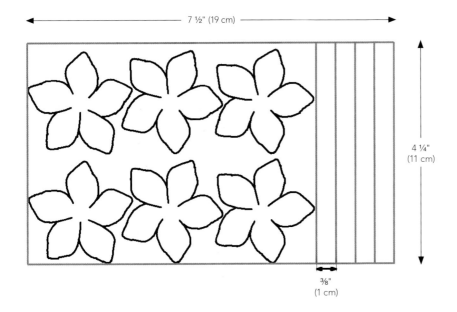

7 ½" (19 cm)

4 ¼" (11 cm)

⅜" (1 cm)

Make the petals.

Using the 2-groove chrysanthemum tool head, iron the petals, as shown in the diagram. Cut a cross in the center of each petal.

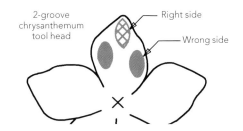

2-groove chrysanthemum tool head — Right side — Wrong side

Make the stamens.

Divide the polystyrene bead stamens into six units, each with approximately 20 stamens. Following the instructions on page 65, secure the 20 stamens with floral stem wire. Wrap floral tape around the wire, about ⅜"- ¾" (1-2 cm) down the length of the wire. Repeat for each stamen unit.

Assemble the flower.

1. Insert one stamen unit through the center of each petal to make six flowers.

2. Wrap floral tape around the hoop earring finding.

3. Start wrapping the stem fabric around the earring, beginning at the front. After wrapping about ⅜" (1 cm), attach a flower by wrapping the stem fabric over the flower wire. Continue wrapping the stem fabric about ¾" (2 cm), then attach the second flower. Repeat process for the third flower.

4. After all three flowers have been attached, wrap the stem fabric about ⅜" (1 cm), then glue to secure. Repeat this step using the second earring finding and remaining flowers.

16. Bachelor's Button

❀ Shown on page 34
❀ Template on page 152

MATERIALS

4" × 6" (10 × 15 cm) shiny satin fabric

4 ¼" × 6" (11 × 15 cm) cotton print fabric

6 plush stamens

3 ½" (9 cm)-long floral stem wire

Floral tape

TOOLS

Flower iron

Knife tool head

Quick-dry tacky glue

Cut the fabric.

Trace and cut out the petal template on page 152.

CUT OUT THE FOLLOWING PIECES:

6 petals of shiny satin fabric

6 petals of cotton print fabric

⅜" × 6" (1 × 15 cm) piece of cotton print fabric for stem

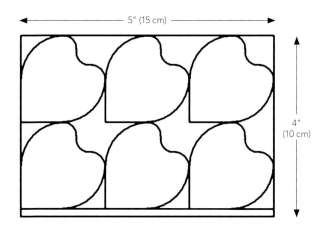

Make the petals.

1. Cut a sawtooth edge into the top of each petal by making cuts about ⅜" (1 cm) deep.

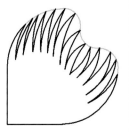

2. Using the knife tool head, iron each petal, as shown in the diagram.

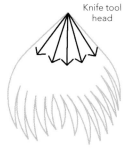

3. Curl the sawtooth edge of each petal using a sharp pair of scissors.

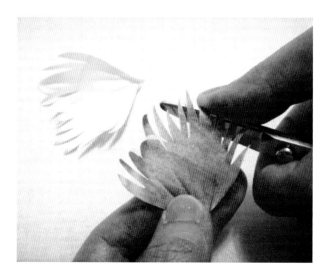

Make the stamen.

Following the instructions on page 65, secure six stamens with floral stem wire. Wrap floral tape around the wire, about 1 ¼"-1 ½" (3-4 cm) down the length of the wire.

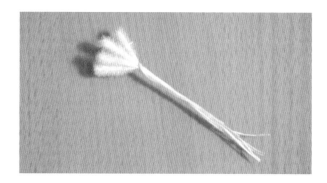

Assemble the flower.

1. Apply glue to the base of each petal. Attach petals to the underside of the stamens, making sure to slightly overlap each petal. Use 3 petals for the first row, 3 petals for the second row, and 6 petals for the third row. Mix the satin and cotton print petals to achieve desired look.

2. Trim the stem wire to 1 ¼" (3 cm). Wrap the stem fabric around the wire and secure with glue. Adjust the petals.

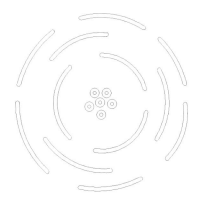

17. Double Impatiens

❃ Shown on page 35
❃ Templates on page 153

MATERIALS

4 ¾" × 4 ¾" (12 × 12 cm) silk fabric for flower

3" × 15 ½" (7.5 × 39 cm) silk fabric for headband

1 ⅜" (3.5 cm)-wide plastic headband

86" (218 cm) of ⅝" (1.5 cm)-wide satin ribbon

Three 4 ¾" (12 cm)-long floral stem wires

TOOLS

Flower iron

Large spoon tool head

Quick-dry tacky glue

Needle

Invisible thread

Cut the fabric.

Trace and cut out the headband, small, medium, and large petal templates on page 153.

CUT OUT THE FOLLOWING PIECES:

2 small petals of silk fabric for flower

2 medium petals of silk fabric for flower

2 large petals of silk fabric for flower

1 headband piece of silk fabric for headband (cut on fold)

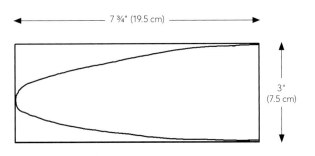

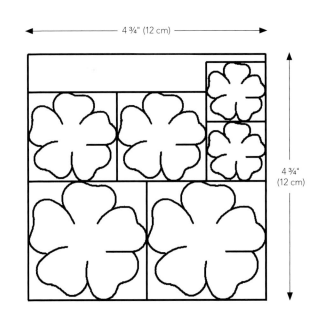

Make the petals.

Using the large spoon tool head, iron each petal, as shown in the diagram. Cut two parallel slits in the center of one small petal. Cut a cross in the center of all the other petals.

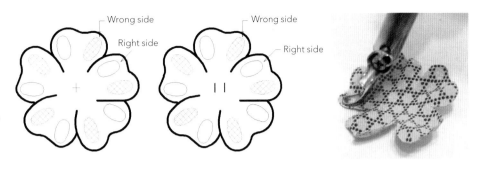

Assemble the flower.

1. Bend all three floral stem wires in half. Insert the wires through both slits in the small petal with two parallel slits. Secure with glue.

2. Apply glue to the center of each petal. Insert the stem wires through the cross slit in each petal, starting with the other small petal, then the medium petals, then the large petals.

Make the headband.

1. Apply glue to the underside of the headband. Center the fabric and adhere to the underside of the headband. Fold the remainder of the fabric to the top of the headband and adhere.

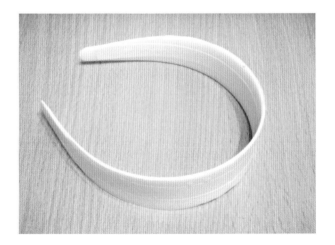

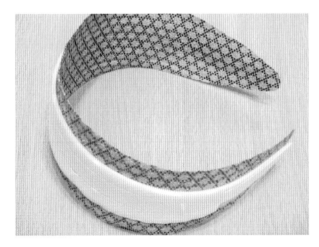

2. Fold the fabric ends to the top of the headband. Cover these ends and the seam at the top of the headband with satin ribbon.

3. Use the remaining ribbon to make a bow, as shown on page 65.

4. Attach the bow to the headband using glue.

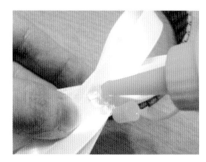 

5. Trim excess stem wires. Apply glue to the base of the flower and attach it to the bow on the headband.

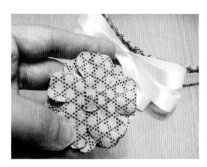 

18. Tuberose

❀ Shown on page 36
❀ Templates on page 154

MATERIALS

5" × 8" (13 × 20.5 cm) velvet fabric for flower

⅜" × 15 ½" (1 × 39 cm) velvet fabric for headband top

⅕"x 15 ½" (0.5 × 39 cm) velvet fabric for headband underside

Three pearl stamens

One ¼" (0.7 cm)-wide plastic headband

Two 4 ¾" (12 cm)-long floral stem wires

Floral tape

TOOLS

Flower iron   Quick-dry tacky glue

Large spoon tool head   Hot glue gun

Cut the fabric.

Trace and cut out the petal and leaf templates on page 154.

CUT OUT THE FOLLOWING PIECES:

Two 1 ½" × 4 ¾" (4 × 12 cm) pieces of velvet fabric for the petals.

Two 2 ½" × 2 ½" (6.5 × 6.5 cm) pieces of velvet fabric for the leaves

2 leaves of velvet fabric

⅕" (0.5 cm)-wide length of velvet fabric for the stem

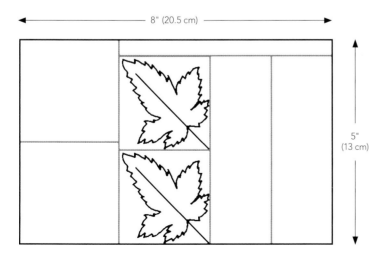

Make the petals.

1. Apply tacky glue to the wrong side of one of the 1 ½" × 4 ¾" (4 × 12 cm) pieces. Place second piece of fabric on top with right side facing up. Cut into three equal pieces.

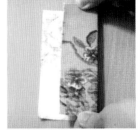

2. Using the petal template, cut out 3 petals from the double fabric. Make ⅛" (0.5 cm)-deep cuts between individual petals. Cut a cross in the center of each petal.

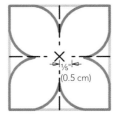

—⅛" (0.5 cm)

3. Using the large spoon tool head, iron the petals, as shown in the diagram.

Large spoon tool head

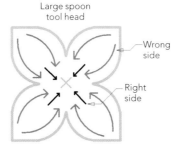

Wrong side

Right side

Make the leaves.

1. Apply tacky glue to the wrong side of each leaf. Press a floral stem wire into the glue, then place a 2 ½" × 2 ½" (6.5 × 6.5 cm) piece on top of each leaf with right side facing up. Trim excess fabric.

2. Using the large spoon tool head, iron the leaves, as shown in the diagrams below.

Large spoon tool head
Right side

Large spoon tool head
Wrong side

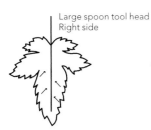
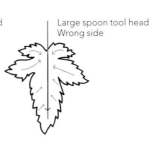

Assemble the flowers.

Insert one stamen through the cross in the center of each petal and secure with tacky glue.

Make the headband.

1. Wrap the headband in floral tape.

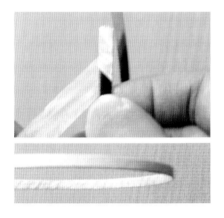

2. Apply tacky glue to the wrong side of the ⅜" × 15 ½" (1 × 39 cm) piece of velvet and adhere to the top of the headband, leaving ⅜" (1 cm) excess at each end. Fold the excess fabric to the underside of the headband and secure.

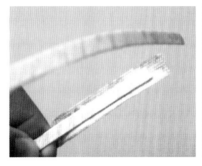

3. Apply tacky glue to the underside of headband and adhere the ⅛" × 15 ½" (0.5 × 39 cm) piece of velvet.

4. Arrange the flowers and leaves. Trim the stem wires to ⅜"- ¾" (1-2 cm) and wrap with floral tape.

5. Wrap the stem fabric around the stem wires and glue to secure. Attach the flower to the headband using a hot glue gun.

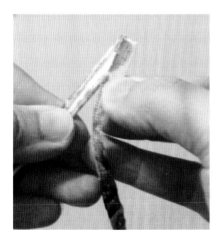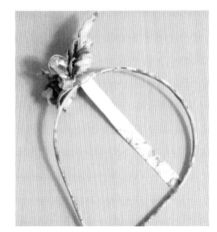

19. Zinnia

❧ Shown on page 37
❧ Templates on page 154

MATERIALS

6 ½" × 6 ½" (16.5 × 16.5 cm) of waffle-weave fabric

6 ½" × 6 ½" (6.5 × 16.5 cm) of voile fabric

2" × 8" (5 × 20 cm) of light-colored cotton slub fabric

1 ¼" × 8" (3 × 20 cm) of dark-colored cotton slub fabric

3 ½" (9 cm)-long floral stem wire

20 glass beads

TOOLS

Flower iron   Medium spoon tool head   Quick-dry tacky glue

Cut the fabric.

Trace and cut out templates on page 154.*

CUT OUT THE FOLLOWING PIECES:

2 small petals of waffle-weave fabric

2 large petals of waffle-weave fabric

2 small petals of voile fabric

2 large petals of voile fabric

1" × 8" (2.5 × 20 cm) piece of light-colored cotton slub fabric for the inner petals**

⅝" × 8" (1.5 × 20 cm) of light-colored cotton slub fabric for the stamen**

⅝" × 8" (1.5 × 20 cm) of dark-colored cotton slub fabric for the stamen**

*Make sure to position templates in the same direction for both fabrics.
**No diagram for these pieces. Cut according to dimensions listed above.

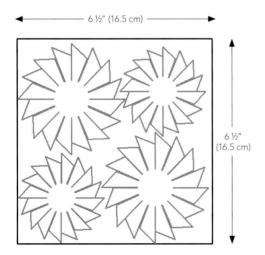

Waffle-Weave Fabric

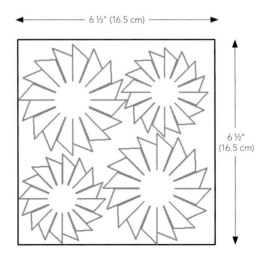

Voile Fabric

Make the petals.

1. Using the medium spoon tool head, iron each waffle-weave petal on the wrong side, as shown in the diagram. After ironing, glue the corresponding voile petal to the wrong side of each waffle-weave petal, applying glue to the center of the petals only. Cut a cross in the center of each petal.

2. To make the inner petals, cut a sawtooth edge into the 1" × 8" (2.5 × 20 cm) piece of light-colored cotton slub fabric, making cuts about ¾" (2 cm)-deep and ⅜" (1 cm) apart.

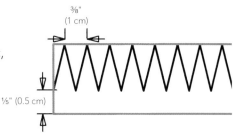
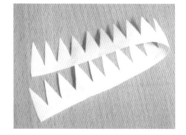

3. Apply glue to the sawtooth edge tips and twist. Apply more glue and insert each tip through a glass bead.

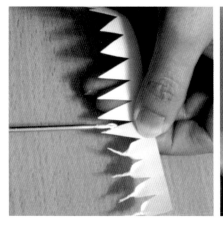
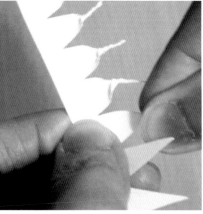
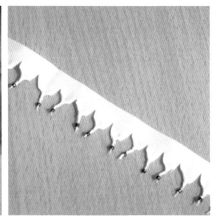

Make the stamens.

1. Apply glue to the wrong side of each ⅝" x 8" (1.5 x 20 cm) piece of cotton slub fabric. Attach the light-colored piece to the dark-colored piece. Make ⅜" (1 cm)-deep cuts about ¹⁄₁₆" (0.2 cm) apart.

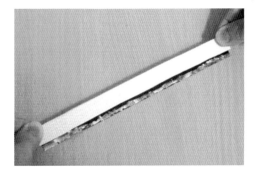

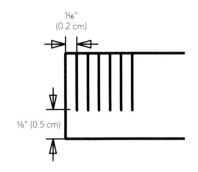

¹⁄₁₆"
(0.2 cm)

⅛" (0.5 cm)

2. Bend one floral stem wire in half. Insert into one end of the fringe strip. Apply glue to the fabric and wrap it around the wire in a spiral.

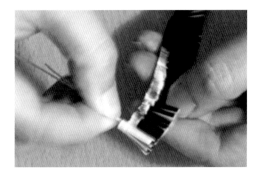

Assemble the flower.

1. Apply glue to the straight edge of the sawtooth piece and wrap it around the stamen piece.

2. Apply glue to the center of each petal. Assemble each flower by inserting the stamen wire through the center of two small petals, then two large petals.

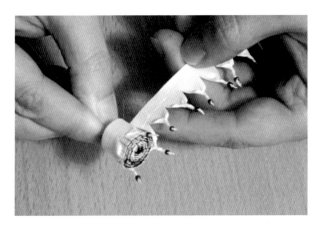

20. Freesia

❀ Shown on page 38
❀ Templates on page 154

MATERIALS

9" × 9 ¾" (22 × 24.5 cm) velvet fabric

9" × 9 ¾" (22 × 24.5 cm) embroidered lace fabric with small floral motifs

12 black pearl stamens

Six 7" (18 cm)-long floral stem wires

15 ¾" (40 cm) of 6 mm plastic tubing

Floral tape

TOOLS

Flower iron

Large spoon tool head

Quick-dry tacky glue

Cut the fabric.

Cut out 12 floral motifs from the embroidered lace fabric. Trace and cut out the A and B petal and A, B, and C leaf templates on page 154.

CUT OUT THE FOLLOWING PIECES:

6 A petals of velvet fabric

6 B petals of velvet fabric

2 A leaves of velvet fabric

2 B leaves of velvet fabric

2 C leaves of velvet fabric

1 ¾" (4.5 cm)-wide lengths of velvet fabric for the stems

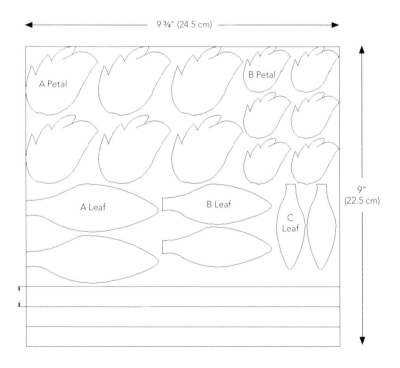

Make the stamens.

Divide the stamens into two equal groups. Following the instructions on page 65, secure the stamens with wire. Cut the plastic tubing into five equal lengths.

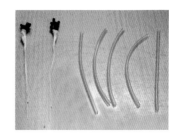

Make the petals.

1. Apply glue to the embroidered lace floral motifs and adhere one to the wrong side of each velvet petal.

2. Using the large spoon tool head, iron the A and B petals on the right side, as shown in the diagram. Follow the diagram to create raised grain.

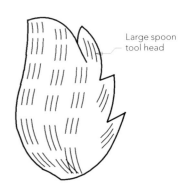

Large spoon tool head

Make the leaves.

1. Lay out three sets of leaves (A-C), each with a top and bottom. Apply glue to the center of each bottom leaf. Press a floral stem wire into the glue, leaving a ⅜" (1 cm) space at the top of each piece. Add each top leaf, making sure glue adheres to both leaf pieces in the set. Make three sets (A-C). Twist the edges of the leaves to shape.

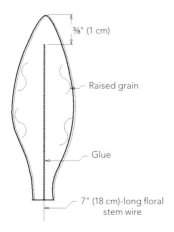

⅜" (1 cm)

Raised grain

Glue

7" (18 cm)-long floral stem wire

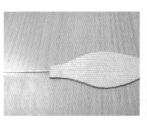

2. Trim any excess fabric from the leaf base. Wrap the wires with floral tape, then insert each wire into a piece of plastic tubing. Wrap the tubing with floral tape.

3. Wrap the stem fabric around the tubing and secure with glue.

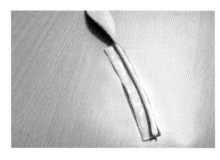 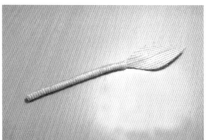

Assemble the flower.

1. Apply glue to the base of each petal. Attach the 3 A petals to the underside of one group of stamens. Attach the 3 B petals to the underside of the other group of stamens.

   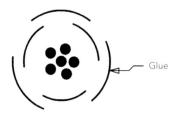

Glue

2. Arrange the two flowers and three leaves and fasten with wire. Wrap the wire with a piece of stem fabric.

21. Rosa Rugosa

❉ Shown on page 40
❉ Templates on page 155

MATERIALS

9" × 15" (23 × 38 cm) voile fabric

20 long pearl stamens

Thirteen 4 ¾" (12 cm)-long floral stem wires

Floral tape

TOOLS

Flower iron

24 mm radius tool head

Large spoon tool head

Quick-dry tacky glue

Cut the fabric.

Trace and cut out the calyx, small, medium, and large petal templates on page 155.

CUT OUT THE FOLLOWING PIECES:

1 calyx of voile fabric

6 small petals of voile fabric

8 medium petals of voile fabric

10 large petals of voile fabric

⅜" (1 cm)-wide lengths of voile fabric for stems

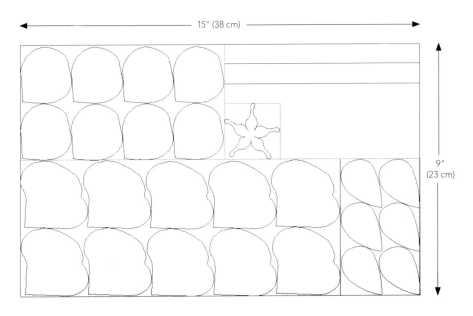

Make the stamens.

Following the instructions on page 65, secure 20 stamens with floral stem wire. When completed, stamens should be 1 ¼" (3 cm) in length. Wrap and glue the stem fabric about ⅜"- ¾" (1-2 cm) down then length of the wire.

Make the petals.

1. Lay out sets of petals, each with a top and bottom piece. Apply glue to the remaining floral stem wires. Place each wire in the center of each bottom petal, leaving a ⅜" (1 cm) space at the top of each bottom petal. Add each top petal, making sure glue adheres to both petal pieces in the set. Make 3 wired small petals, 4 wired medium petals, and 5 wired large petals.

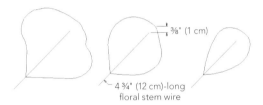

⅜" (1 cm)

4 ¾" (12 cm)-long floral stem wire

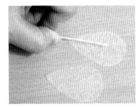

2. Using the 24 mm radius tool head, iron the wired small and medium petals, as shown in the diagram. Using both the 24 mm radius tool head and the large spoon tool head, iron each wired large petal, as shown in the diagram.

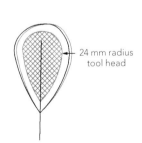

24 mm radius tool head

24 mm radius tool head

Right side

Wrong side

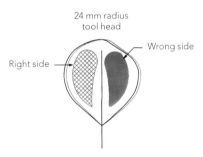

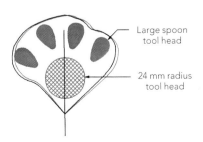

Large spoon tool head

24 mm radius tool head

Assemble the flower.

1. Apply glue to the base of each petal. Attach petals to the underside of the stamens. Use small petals for the first row, medium petals for the second row, and large petals for the third row.

2. Wrap floral tape around the stem wires, about 2"-2 ½" (5-6 cm) down the length of the wires. Trim excess wire.

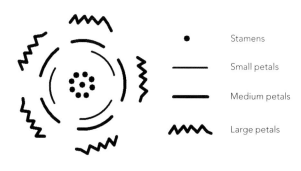

3. Cut a slit in the center of the calyx. Insert the stem wire through the calyx and glue the calyx to the back of the assembled flower. Wrap and glue the stem fabric around the stem wire.

22. *Tulip Poplar*

❋ Shown on page 42
❋ Templates on page 155

MATERIALS

5" × 6 ¼" (12.5 × 16 cm) cotton fabric

6" × 6 ¼" (15.5 × 16 cm) shiny satin fabric

1 pearl stamen

Three 4 ¾" (12 cm)-long floral stem wires

Floral tape

TOOLS

Flower iron

21 mm radius tool head

Quick-dry tacky glue

Cut the fabric.

Cut out a 4 ½" × 6 ¼" (11.5 × 16 cm) piece of each fabric. Glue these two pieces with wrong sides together. Allow to dry to dampness—do not dry completely. Trace and cut out the calyx, petal, and leaf templates on page 155.

CUT OUT THE FOLLOWING PIECES:

1 calyx of damp double fabric

2 petals of damp double fabric

1 ½" × 4 ¾" (4 × 12 cm) piece of damp double fabric for stamen

⅜" × 6 ¼" (1 × 16 cm) of damp double fabric for the stem

Two 1 ½" × 3 ⅛" (4 × 8 cm) pieces of shiny satin fabric for the leaves

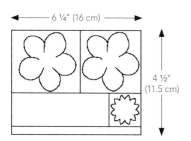

Damp Double Fabric

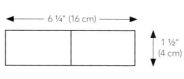

Shiny Satin Fabric

Make the stamen.

Fold the 1 ½" × 4 ¾" (4 × 12 cm) piece of damp double fabric in half lengthwise and glue together at the bottom edge. Make ⅝" (1.5 cm)-deep cuts, about ⅕" (0.5 cm) apart into the folded top edge. Apply glue to the bottom edge and wrap it around the stamen in a spiral.

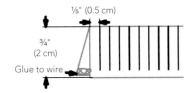

Make the leaves.

1. Fold one of the 1 ½" × 3 ⅛" (4 × 8 cm) pieces of shiny satin fabric in half widthwise. Apply glue to the wrong side of the fabric and attach two floral stem wires to the center of each leaf, leaving a ⅝" (1.5 cm) space at the top of each leaf. Place second piece of satin fabric on top with right side facing up. Allow to dry. Cut on the fold line for a total of two wired pieces. Using leaf template, trim the wired pieces to create two leaves.

2. Make ⅜" (1 cm)-deep cuts, about ⅛" (3 mm) apart around the edges of each leaf.

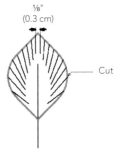

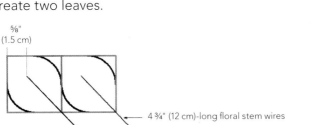

3. Using the 21 mm radius tool head, iron the leaves, as shown in the diagram.

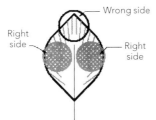

Make the petals and calyx.

Using the 21 mm radius tool head, iron the petals and calyx on the right side, as shown in the diagram. Cut a cross in the center of each petal and the calyx.

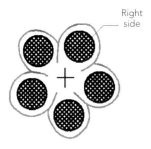

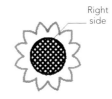

Assemble the flower.

1. Apply glue to the center of each petal. Insert the stamen through each petal. Insert the stamen through the calyx and glue the calyx to the back of the assembled flower.

2. Arrange the flower and leaves. Wrap the stem wires with floral tape, about ¾"-1 ¼" (2-3 cm) down the length of the wires. Trim excess wire. Wrap the stem fabric around the group of wires and glue to secure.

23. Ranunculus

❀ Shown on page 44
❀ Templates on page 156

MATERIALS

2" × 9 ½" (5 × 24 cm) cotton fabric

19" (48 cm) of 2" (5 cm)-wide sheer ribbon

50 small pearl stamens

7" (18 cm)-long floral stem wire

Ring base

TOOLS

Flower iron

16 mm radius tool head

Quick-dry tacky glue

Hot glue gun

Cut the fabric.

Cut the ribbon in half into two 9 ½" (24 cm)-long pieces. Apply tacky glue to the wrong side of both pieces of ribbon and adhere to both sides of the piece of cotton fabric. Trace and cut out the petal and calyx templates on page 156.

CUT OUT THE FOLLOWING PIECES:

4 petals of ribbon fabric

1 calyx of ribbon fabric

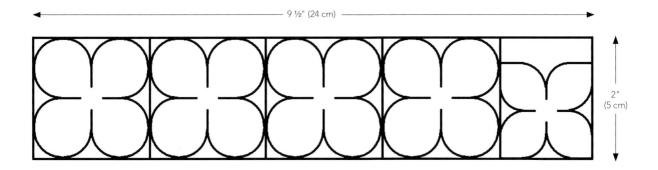

Make the petals.

1. Cut each petal into four pieces.

2. Fold the rounded top edge of each petal piece back ⅜" (1 cm). Using the 16 mm radius tool head, iron the bottom of each petal, as shown in the diagram.

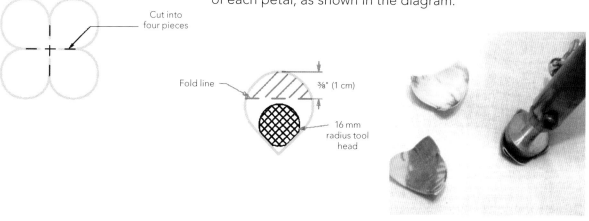

Make the stamens.

Following the instructions on page 65, secure 50 stamens with floral stem wire. When completed, stamens should be ⅝" (1.5 cm) in length.

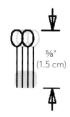

Assemble the flower.

Apply tacky glue to the underside of the stamens and attach four petal pieces, making sure to slightly overlap each petal piece. Attach all remaining petal pieces, making sure to spiral and overlap each petal piece. Insert the stamen wire through the calyx and glue the calyx to the back of the assembled flower. Trim excess wire. Attach the flower to the ring base using a hot glue gun.

24. Anemone

MATERIALS

3 ½" × 9 ½" (9 × 24 cm) linen fabric

⅝" (1.5 cm) polystyrene ball

7" (18 cm)-long floral stem wire

31 2.5 mm in diameter sequins

31 short straight pins

TOOLS

Flower iron

10 mm radius tool head

16 mm radius tool head

21 mm radius tool head

Quick-dry tacky glue

❀ Shown on page 45

❀ Templates on page 156

Cut the fabric.

Trace and cut out the calyx, small, medium, and large petal templates on page 156.

CUT OUT THE FOLLOWING PIECES:

1 calyx of linen fabric

3 small petals of linen fabric

4 medium petals of linen fabric

5 large petals of linen fabric

1 ½" × 1 ½" (4 × 4 cm) piece of linen fabric for the stamen

9 ½" (24 cm)

1 ½" (4 cm)

1 ½" (4 cm)

3 ½" (9 cm)

Make the petals.

Use the 10 mm radius tool head for the small petals, the 16 mm radius tool head for the medium petals, and the 21 mm radius tool head for the large petals. Fold each petal in half with right sides together and iron one half of the petal on the wrong side, as shown in the diagram. Unfold each petal and iron the other half of the petal on the wrong side, as shown in the diagram.

Fold in half

Make the calyx.

Cut a Y-shaped slit in the center of the calyx.

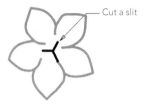

Cut a slit

Make the stamen.

1. Insert a floral stem wire through the polystyrene ball, bend the wire, and twist to secure. Trim the 1 ½" × 1 ½" (4 × 4 cm) piece of linen fabric into a circle. Apply glue on the wrong side of the fabric and wrap it around the polystyrene ball. Trim excess fabric.

2. Insert a pin through the hole of a sequin, then into the ball. Repeat process with remaining pins and sequins until entire ball is covered.

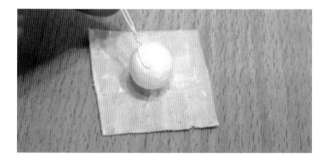 

Assemble the flower.

Apply glue to the base of each petal. Attach petals to the underside of the stamen. Use the small petals for the first row, medium petals for the second row, and large petals for the third row. Make sure to attach the small petals concavely and medium and large petals convexly. Insert the stamen wire through the calyx and glue the calyx to the back of the assembled flower. Trim excess wire.

25. Miniature Rose

MATERIALS

7" × 8" (18 × 20 cm) cotton slub fabric

3" × 8" (7.5 × 20 cm) print fabric

1 teardrop-shaped polystyrene ball

Four 7" (18 cm)-long floral stem wires

Floral tape

TOOLS

Flower iron

21 mm radius tool head

Rat tail tool head

Knife tool head

Quick-dry tacky glue

❀ Shown on page 46
❀ Templates on page 156

Cut the fabric.

Trace and cut out the calyx, leaf, small, medium and large petal templates on page 156.

CUT OUT THE FOLLOWING PIECES:

1 calyx of cotton slub fabric

3 small petals of cotton slub fabric

3 medium petals of cotton slub fabric

5 large petals of cotton slub fabric

Two 1 ¾" × 5 ½" (4.5 × 14 cm) pieces of cotton slub fabric for the leaves

2" × 2" (5 × 5 cm) triangle of cotton slub fabric for the stamen

⅜" (1 cm)-wide lengths of cotton slub fabric for the stems

3 small petals of print fabric

3 medium petals of print fabric

5 large petals of print fabric

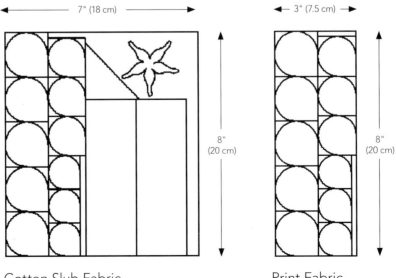

Cotton Slub Fabric

Print Fabric

Make the leaves.

1. Fold one of the 1 ¾" × 5 ½" (4.5 × 14 cm) pieces of cotton slub fabric into thirds and crease. Apply glue to the wrong side of the fabric and attach three floral stem wires to the center of each leaf, leaving a ⅕" (0.5 cm) space at the top of each leaf. Place second piece of cotton slub fabric on top with right side facing up. Allow to dry. Cut on the fold lines for a total of three wired pieces. Using leaf template, trim the wired pieces to create three leaves.

2. Using the knife tool head, iron each leaf on the right side, as shown in the diagram.

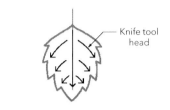

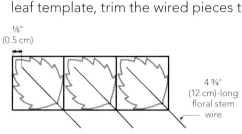

⅕"
(0.5 cm)

4 ¾"
(12 cm)-long
floral stem
wire

Make the stamen.

1. Insert a floral stem wire through the polystyrene ball, bend the wire, and twist to secure.

2. Fold long edge of the triangle back ⅕" (0.5 cm) to the wrong side. Apply glue to the wrong side of the triangle piece and cover the polystyrene ball, as shown in the diagram.

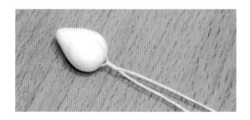

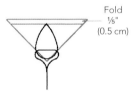

Fold
⅕"
(0.5 cm)

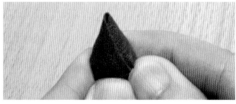

Make the petals.

1. Using the 21 mm radius tool head, iron the base of each petal on the right side, as shown in the diagram.

2. Using the rat tail tool head, iron the edges of each petal on the wrong side, as shown in the diagram.

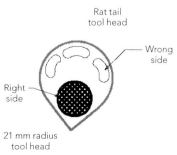

Rat tail
tool head

Wrong
side

Right
side

21 mm radius
tool head

3. Apply glue to the wrong side of each print fabric petal at the base. Place each corresponding print fabric petal on top of each cotton slub fabric petal, leaving a ⅛"-⅕" (0.3-0.5 cm) overlap.

Assemble the flower.

1. Apply glue to the base of each petal. Attach petals to the underside of the stamen. Use small petals for the first row, medium petals for the second row, and large petals for the third row. Cut a slit in the center of the calyx. Insert the stamen through the calyx and glue the calyx to the back of the assembled flower.

Stamens
Small petals
Medium petals
Large petals

2. Wrap and glue the stem fabric around one of the leaf stems, about ⅜"- ¾" (1-2 cm). Add the other two leaves and continue to wrap and glue the stem fabric around the wires.

3. Arrange the flower and leaves. Wrap the group of wires with floral tape, about 1 ½"-2" (4-5 cm) down the length of the wires. Trim excess wire. Wrap the stem fabric around the group of wires and secure with glue.

26. Cosmos

MATERIALS

4 ¼" × 9 ½" (11 × 24 cm) print fabric

11 plastic stamens

Three 7" (18 cm)-long floral stem wires

3 ¼" (8 cm) spring barrette

TOOLS

Flower iron

Small spoon tool head

Quick-dry tacky glue

❀ Shown on page 47
❀ Templates on page 157

Cut the fabric.

Trace and cut out the templates on page 157.

CUT OUT THE FOLLOWING PIECES:

4 large petals of print fabric

2 small petals of print fabric

¾" × 3 ½" (2 × 9 cm) piece of print fabric for barrette top

⅜" × 2 ¼" (1 × 5.5 cm) piece of print fabric for barrette bottom

⅕" (0.5 cm)-wide lengths of print fabric for stems

⅜" (1 cm)-wide length of print fabric for stem

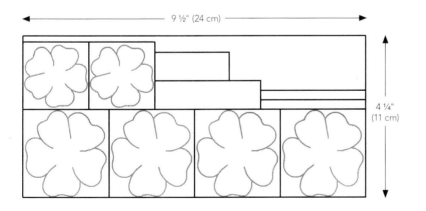

Make the petals.

Using the small spoon tool head, iron the petals on the wrong side, as shown in the diagram. Cut a cross in the center of each petal.

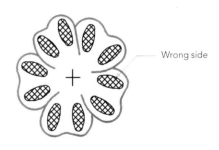

Wrong side

Make the petals.

Using the medium spoon tool head, iron the petals and the tri-petal flower as shown in the diagram.

Small and
Medium
Petals

Large
Petals

Make the leaves.

Using the medium spoon tool head, iron the leaves, as shown in the diagram.

Right side

Wrong side

Make the stamen.

1. Cut a pointed edge into the ⅝" × 7 ¾" (1.5 × 20 cm) piece. Make ⅜" (1 cm)-deep cuts, about ⅜" (1 cm) apart.

⅜" (1 cm)

⅕" (0.5 cm)

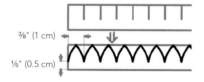

2. Using the medium spoon tool head, iron the stamen piece, as shown in the diagram.

3. Bend the two floral stem wires into loops. Thread the loops over the last two points on the stamen piece. Apply glue to the bottom edge of the stamen piece and wrap it around the wires.

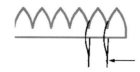

Assemble the flower.

1. Apply glue to the base of each small petal. Attach the small petals to the underside of the stamen.

2. Apply glue to the base of each medium and large petal. Attach the medium petals to the underside of the small petals. Attach the large petals to the underside of the medium petals.

3. Insert the stamen through the calyx and glue the calyx to the back of the assembled flower. Trim excess wires.

4. Thread a pearl bead onto each end of the ribbon and tie a knot to secure.

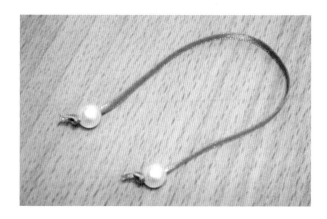

5. Cut a cross in the center of each tri-petal piece. Slip two tri-petal pieces onto each end of the ribbon over the beads. Secure with glue.

6. Attach the leaves to the brooch base using glue. Fold the ribbon unevenly and glue it to the brooch base. Glue the flower to the brooch base.

29. Summer Wine Rose

❁ Shown on page 52
❁ Templates on page 158

MATERIALS

5 ¾" × 11 ¾" (14.5 × 30 cm) voile fabric

11 ¾"x 11 ¾" (30 × 30 cm) cotton fabric

30 large multicolored stamens

7" (18 cm)-long floral stem wire

TOOLS

Flower iron

Forget-me-not tool head

Quick-dry tacky glue

Cut the fabric.

Trace and cut out the calyx, small, medium, and large petal templates on page 158.

CUT OUT THE FOLLOWING PIECES:

16 small petals of cotton fabric

10 medium petals of cotton fabric

10 large petals of cotton fabric

1 calyx of cotton fabric

8 small petals of voile fabric

5 medium petals of voile fabric

5 large petals of voile fabric

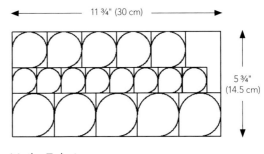

Voile Fabric

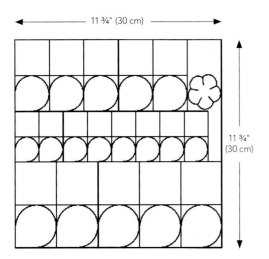

Cotton Fabric

Make the petals.

1. Make a petal set by gluing two cotton petals together, then gluing a voile petal on top. Make sure to glue the petals together at the base only. Make petal sets with all of the petals.

Glue the petals together.

2. Using the forget-me-not tool head, iron the petals, as shown in the diagram. When ironing the small petals, iron four on the voile side and four on the cotton side.

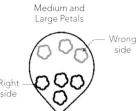

Small Petals

Medium and Large Petals

Wrong side

Right side

Make the calyx.

Using the forget-me-not tool head, iron the calyx on the right side, as shown in the diagram.

Make the stamens.

Following the instructions on page 65, secure the stamens with floral stem wire.

Floral stem wire

Assemble the flower.

Apply glue to the base of each petal. Attach petals to the underside of the stamens. Use the small petals ironed on the cotton side for the first row, the small petals ironed on the voile side for the second row, the medium petals for the third row, and the large petals for the fourth row. Trim excess wire.

- Stamens
— Small petals
— Medium petals
∿ Large petals

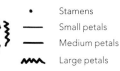

30. English Rose

❀ Shown on page 54
❀ Templates on page 158

MATERIALS

13" × 13" (33 × 33 cm) cotton fabric

Large bunch of tiny stamens

Three 10 mm pearls

Eight 7" (18 cm)-long floral stem wires

Floral tape

TOOLS

Cheesecloth

Quick-dry tacky glue

Cut the fabric.

Trace and cut out the calyx, small, medium, and large petal templates on page 158.

CUT OUT THE FOLLOWING PIECES:

1 calyx of cotton fabric

10 small petals of cotton fabric

10 medium petals of cotton fabric

10 large petals of cotton fabric

⅜" (1 cm)-wide lengths of cotton fabric for the stem

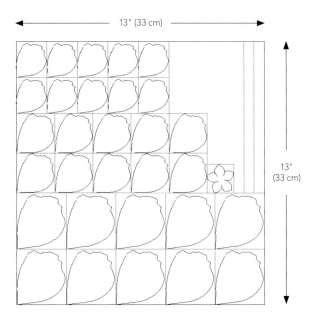

13" (33 cm)

13" (33 cm)

Make the stamens.

1. Cut two strands of the tiny stamens in half. Insert one of these stamen pieces through one of the pearls. Insert a floral stem wire through the opposite end of the pearl. Secure the stamen to the wire with floral tape, wrapping about ¾"-1 ¼" (2-3 cm) down the length of the wire. Repeat this process with the two remaining pearls.

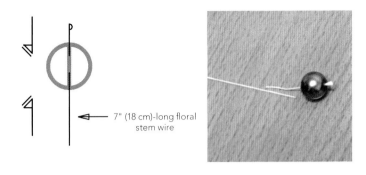

7" (18 cm)-long floral stem wire

2. Fasten the remaining bunch of tiny stamens with floral stem wire around the center. Apply glue to the wired area. Fold the stamen bunch in half.

3. Insert the pearl pieces into the stamen bunch and secure with floral stem wire.

Make the petals.

1. Slightly dampen a petal. Fold the petal in half and place one side on the cheesecloth.

2. Fold the cheesecloth, covering the damp, folded petal. Using the heel of your hand, press and twist the petal to create wrinkles. Allow the petal to dry.

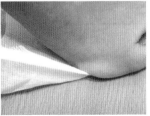

3. Repeat steps 1 and 2 for all petals. Cut the small and medium petals open at the top. The cut should extend to the middle of the petal.

4. Lay out five sets of large petals, each with a top and bottom piece. Glue a floral stem wire to each bottom petal, leaving a ⅜" (1 cm) space at the top. Cover with each top petal. Make five sets.

⅜" (1 cm)

7" (18 cm)-long floral stem wire

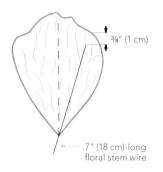

Assemble the flower.

1. Apply glue to the base of each small petal. Attach the small petals to the underside of the stamens. Successive rows of petals will be glued into a spiral around the previous row.

2. Apply glue to the base of each medium and large petal. Attach the medium petals to the underside of the small petals. Attach the large petals to the underside of the medium petals.

3. Insert the stamen through the calyx and glue the calyx to the back of the assembled flower.

4. Wrap the stem wire with floral tape, about 2"-2 ½" (5-6 cm) down the length of the wire. Wrap and glue the stem fabric around the wire.

31. Impatiens

❧ Shown on page 56
❧ Templates on page 159

MATERIALS

6 ¼" × 8" (16 × 20 cm) shiny satin fabric

Two 6 mm rhinestone chatons

3 teardrop-shaped pearls

Fifteen 3" (7.5 cm)-long floral stem wires

8" (20 cm)-long beading wire

TOOLS

Flower iron

Knife tool head

Small spoon tool head

Hammer tool head

Needle

Thread

Quick-dry tacky glue

Cut the fabric.

Trace and cut out the small and large petal templates on page 159.

CUT OUT THE FOLLOWING PIECES:

Two 1 ¼" × 4 ¾" (3 × 12 cm) pieces of shiny satin fabric

Two ¾" × 6 ¼" (2 × 16 cm) pieces of shiny satin

4" × 4 ¾'" (10 × 12 cm) piece of shiny satin for the stolons (long stems)

⅕" (0.5 cm)-wide lengths of shiny satin for the stems

⅜" (1 cm)-wide lengths of shiny satin for the stems

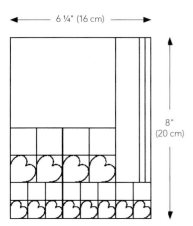

6 ¼" (16 cm)

8"
(20 cm)

Make the petals.

1. Fold one of the 1 ¼" × 4 ¾" (3 × 12 cm) pieces into fourths to crease. Unfold the fabric, apply glue to the wrong side and attach four floral stem wires (one to each section). Place the corresponding piece of satin on top with right side facing up. Cut on fold lines for a total of four wired pieces. Using the large petal template, trim the excess fabric to create four large wired petals.

2. Repeat step 1, folding one of the ¾" × 6 ¼" (2 × 16 cm) pieces into eights, wiring, gluing, and trimming to create eight small wired petals.

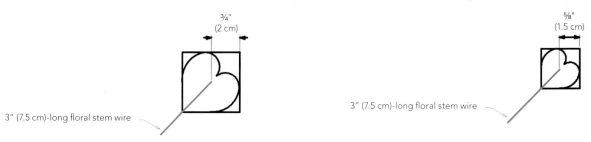

3. Using the knife tool head, iron the petals on the right side, as shown in the diagram. Using the small spoon tool head, iron the petals on the wrong side, as shown in the diagram.

Make the stamens.

1. Insert a 4" (10 cm)-long piece of beading wire through the hole of a rhinestone chaton base. Bend the wire and twist to secure. Repeat with the second rhinestone chaton.

2. Insert a floral stem wire through the hole of a teardrop-shaped pearl. Bend the wire and twist to secure. Repeat with the two remaining pearls.

Make the stolons (long stems).

1. Cut three ½" (1.2 cm)-wide bias strips from the 4" × 4 ¾" (10 × 12 cm) piece of shiny satin.

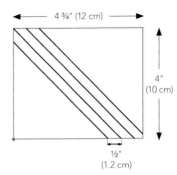

4 ¾" (12 cm)

4" (10 cm)

½" (1.2 cm)

2. With needle and thread, make a stitch slightly in from one edge of a bias strip. Insert the needle through the large hole of the hammer tool head. Gently pull the thread and fabric through the hole to create a tube. Once the tube is complete, cut the thread and neaten the tube ends. Repeat with the remaining two bias strips for a total of three stolons (long stems).

    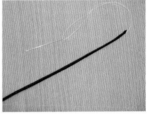

3. Slipstitch a teardrop-shaped pearl to one end of each stolon (long stem). Slipstitch a small petal to the other end of each stolon (long stem). Wrap the ⅕" (0.5 cm)-wide lengths of stem fabric around the wires of two small petals, about 1 ¼"-1 ½" (3-4 cm) down the length of the wires.

Assemble the flower.

1. Glue the three remaining small petals to the underside of one rhinestone stamen to create one flower. Glue the four large petals to the underside of the other rhinestone stamen to create another flower. Wrap and glue the ⅜" (1 cm)-wide lengths of stem fabric around the wires, about 1 ½"-2" (4-5 cm) down the length of the wires.

2. Arrange the small and large flowers with the stolons (long stems). Secure with wire. Cover the wire with a ⅜" (1 cm)-wide length of stem fabric.

32. Dianthus

❀ Shown on page 57
❀ Templates on page 159

MATERIALS

7" × 8 ¾" (18 × 22 cm) of cotton/linen blend fabric

2 ½" × 6" (6 × 15 cm) of cotton slub fabric

5 pearl stamens

7" (18 cm)-long floral stem wire

Floral tape

TOOLS

Flower iron

16 mm radius tool head

Large spoon tool head

Needle

Thread

Quick-dry tacky glue

Cut the fabric.

Trace and cut out the small, large, and wavy petal templates on page 159.

CUT OUT THE FOLLOWING PIECES:

4 small petals of cotton/linen blend fabric*

2 large petals of cotton/linen blend fabric*

⅜" × 1 ¼" (1 × 3 cm) piece of cotton/linen blend fabric

⅝" × 1 ¼" (1.5 × 3 cm) piece of cotton/linen blend fabric

2 wavy petal pieces of cotton slub fabric

*Cut these pieces out along template outlines, not petal outlines.

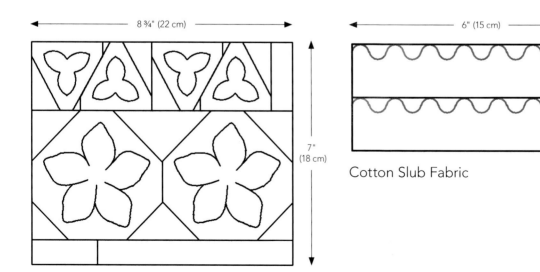

Cotton/Linen Blend Fabric

Cotton Slub Fabric

Make the stamens.

1. For both the ⅜" × 1 ¼" (1 × 3 cm) and ⅝" × 1 ¼" (1.5 × 3 cm) pieces, use tweezers to pull out individual weft (crosswise grain) threads in order to achieve a frayed edge. Pull out weft threads until a ¹⁄₁₆" (0.2 cm) unfrayed edge remains, as shown in diagram.

2. Cut the pearl stamens in half and fasten with floral stem wire.

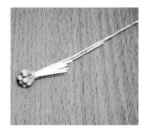

3. Wrap the stem wires with floral tape. Wrap and glue the ⅜" × 1 ¼" (1 × 3 cm) piece, then the ⅝" × 1 ¼" (1.5 × 3 cm) piece around the stamens.

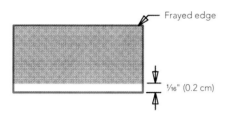

Frayed edge

¹⁄₁₆" (0.2 cm)

Make the petals.

1. Trim the small and large petal templates along petal outlines. Clip or pin the petal templates to the corresponding fabric pieces. Cut slits in the fabric between each petal segment. Use the same process as above to fray the petals until the frayed edge meets the template.

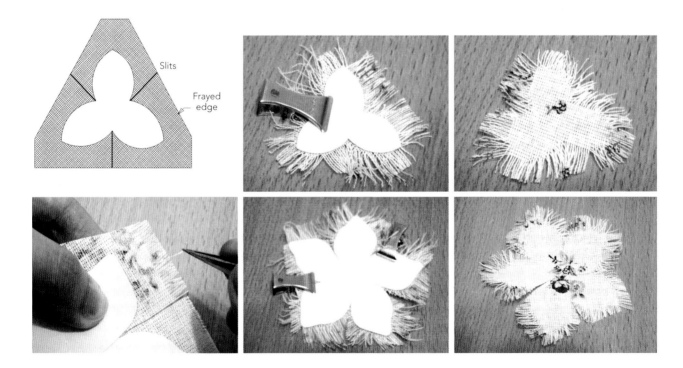

Slits

Frayed edge

2. Using the 16 mm radius tool head, iron the small petals, as shown in the diagram. Using the large spoon tool head, iron the large petals, as shown in the diagram. Cut a cross in the center of each petal.

Small Petals

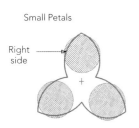

Large Petals

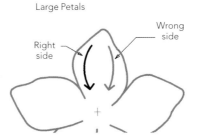

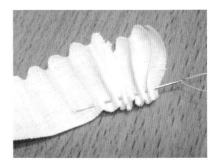

3. Using the large spoon tool head, iron the wavy petal pieces, as shown in the diagram. Sew a running stitch along the base of each wavy petal piece.

Wavy Petal Pieces

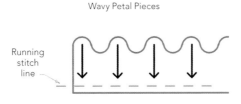

Assemble the flower.

Insert the stamen through the small petals and glue to secure. Glue a wavy petal piece to the underside of the small petals on each side of the flower. Then insert the stamen through the large petals and glue to secure.

Templates

03. Penny Black

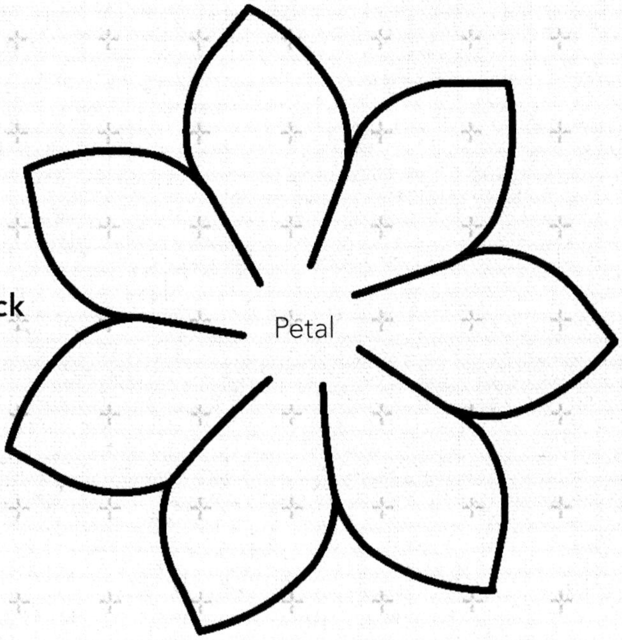

Petal

Small Petal

Large Petal

Medium Petal

04. Shasta Daisy

05. Campanula

Leaf

Ridged Petal

06. Sunflower

Petal

07. Peony

Small Petal

Calyx

Medium Petal

Large Petal

08. Geum Lady Stratheden

Large Petal

Calyx

Small Petal

Medium Petal

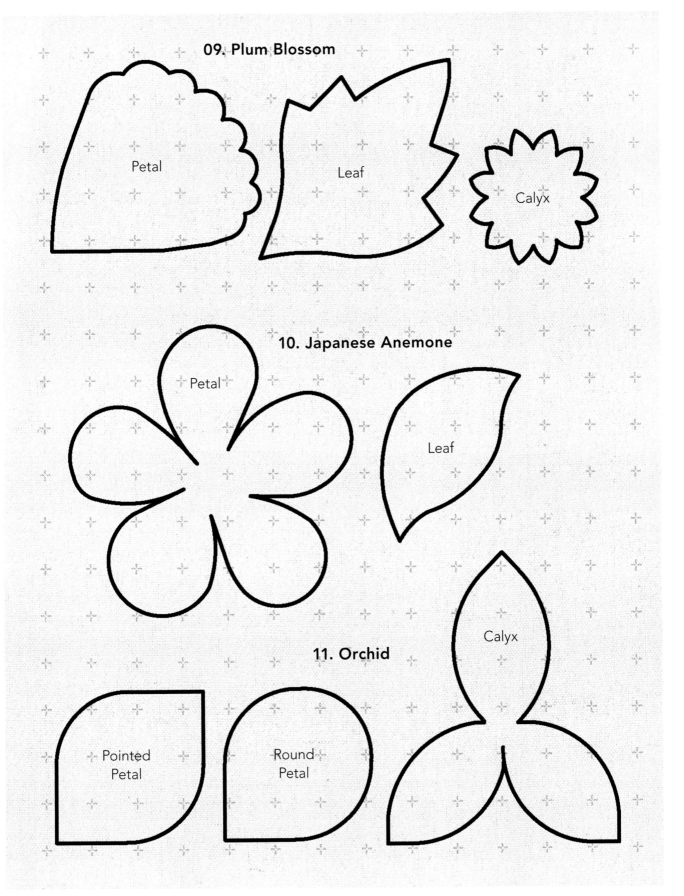

09. Plum Blossom

Petal

Leaf

Calyx

10. Japanese Anemone

Petal

Leaf

11. Orchid

Pointed Petal

Round Petal

Calyx

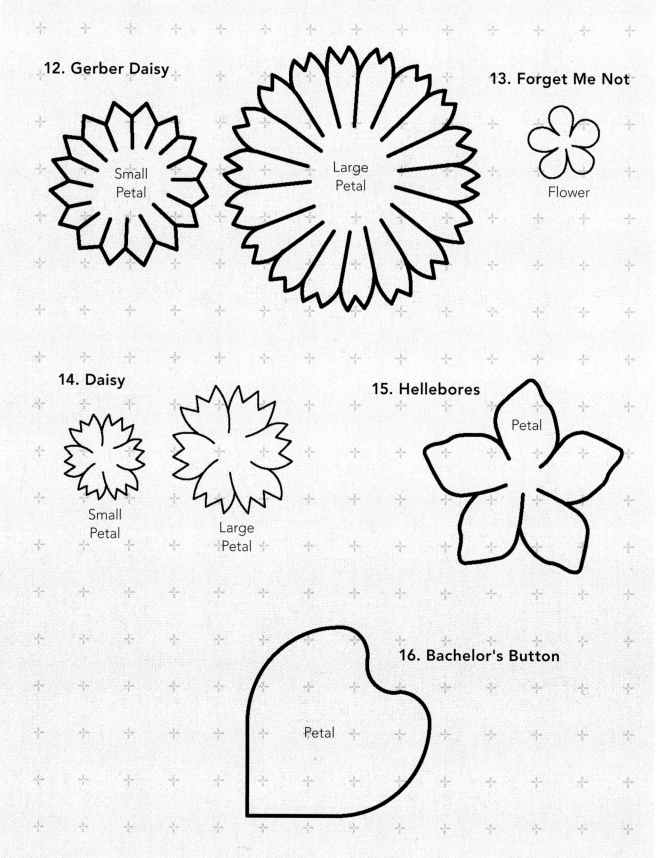

12. Gerber Daisy

Small Petal

Large Petal

13. Forget Me Not

Flower

14. Daisy

Small Petal

Large Petal

15. Hellebores

Petal

16. Bachelor's Button

Petal

17. Double Impatiens

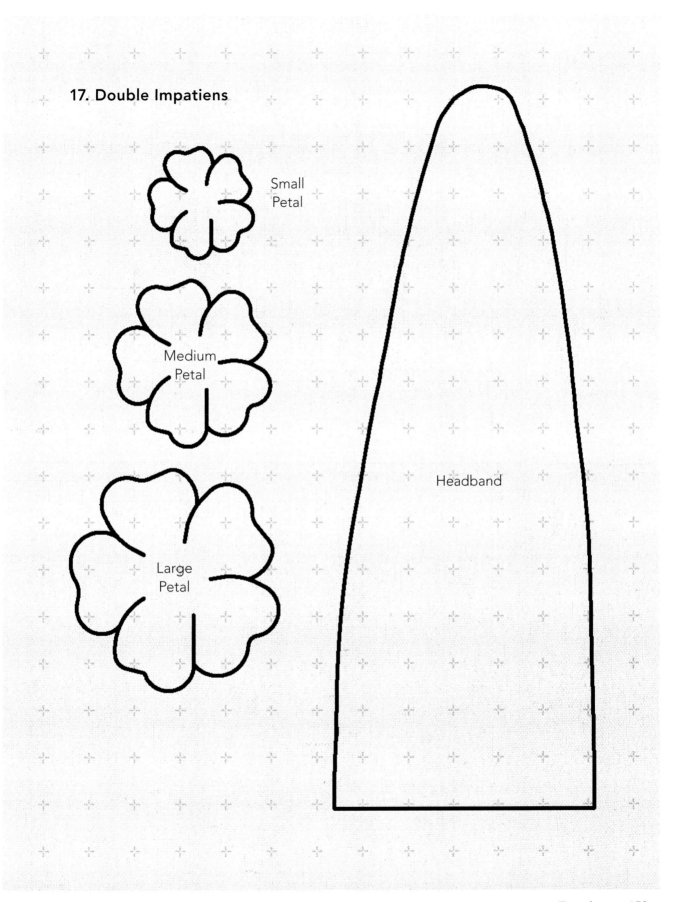

Small Petal

Medium Petal

Large Petal

Headband

Leaf

18. Tuberose

Small
Petal

19. Zinnia

Petal

Large
Petal

20. Freesia

A Leaf

B Leaf

C Leaf

A Petal

B Petal

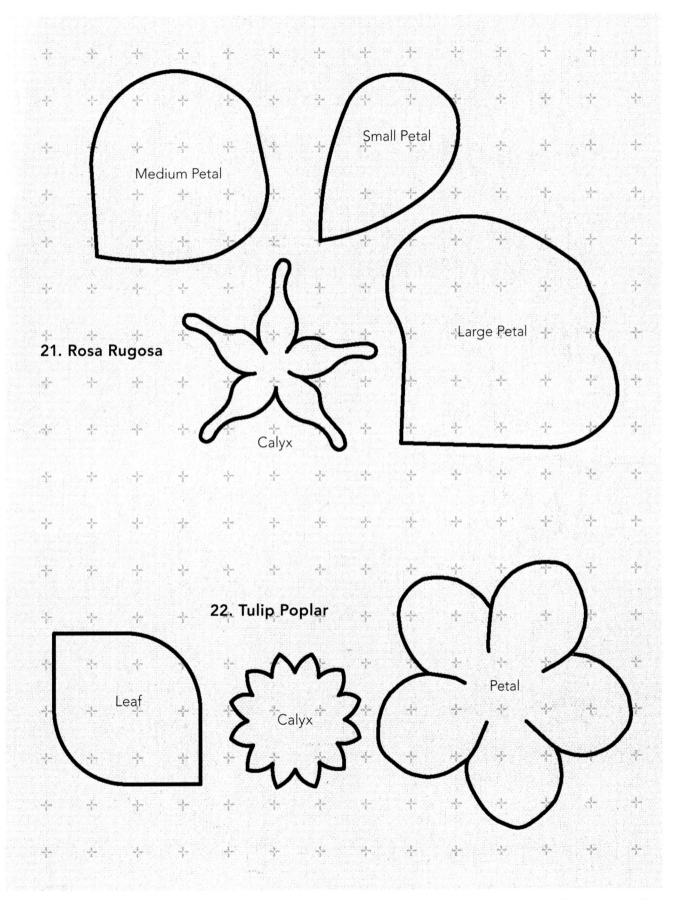

Medium Petal

Small Petal

21. Rosa Rugosa

Calyx

Large Petal

22. Tulip Poplar

Leaf

Calyx

Petal

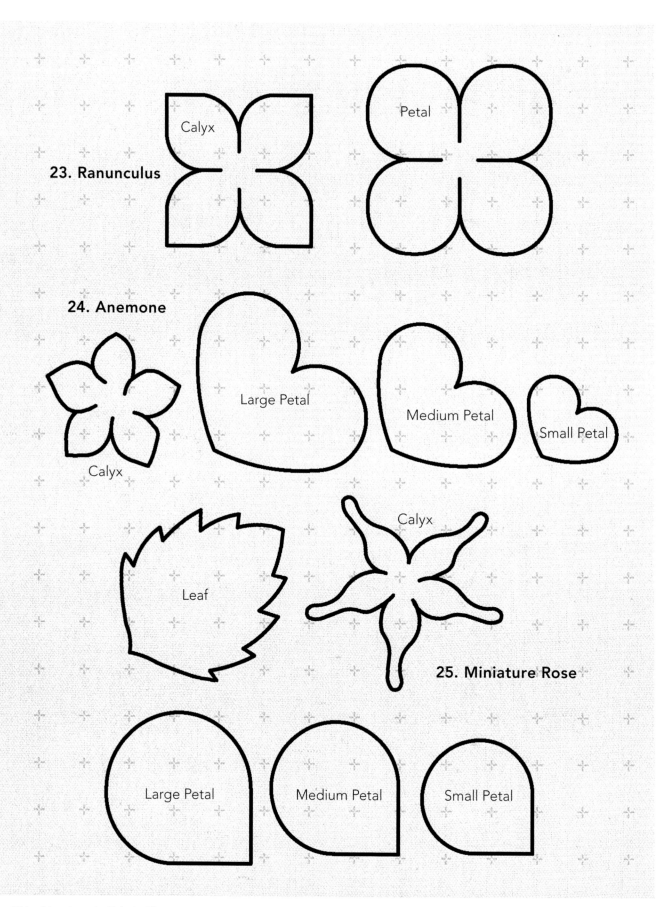

23. Ranunculus

Calyx

Petal

24. Anemone

Calyx

Large Petal

Medium Petal

Small Petal

Leaf

Calyx

25. Miniature Rose

Large Petal

Medium Petal

Small Petal

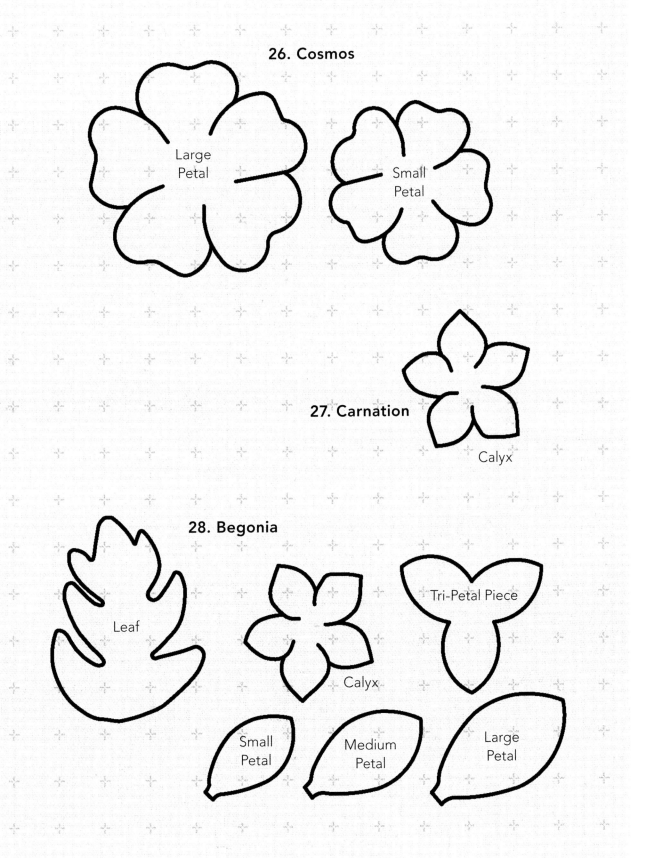

26. Cosmos

Large Petal

Small Petal

27. Carnation

Calyx

28. Begonia

Leaf

Calyx

Tri-Petal Piece

Small Petal

Medium Petal

Large Petal

29. Summer Wine Rose

Large Petal

Calyx

Medium Petal

Small Petal

30. English Rose

Medium Petal

Calyx

Large Petal

Small Petal

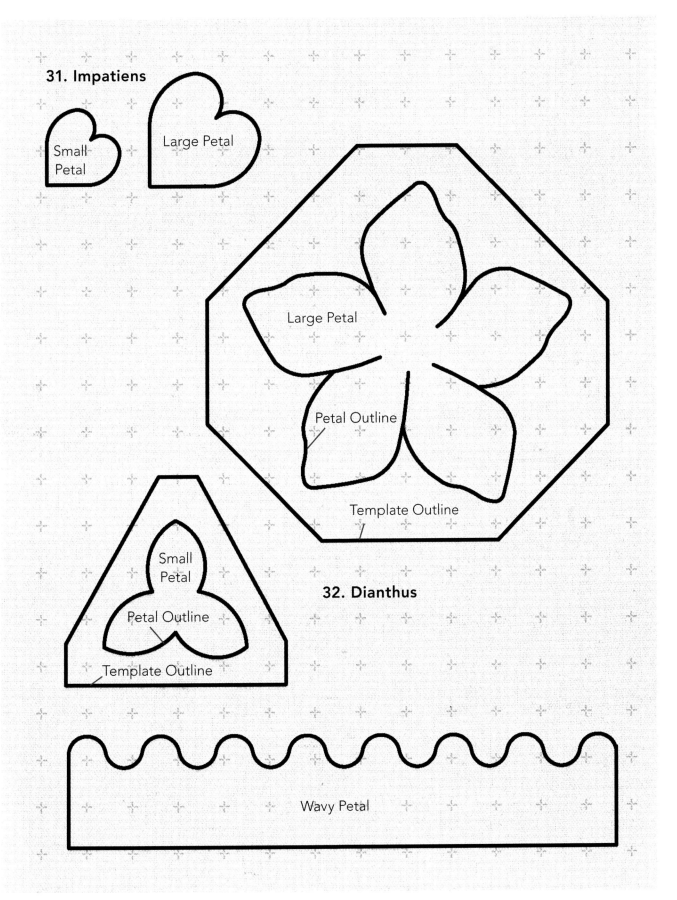

31. Impatiens

Small Petal

Large Petal

Large Petal

Petal Outline

Template Outline

32. Dianthus

Small Petal

Petal Outline

Template Outline

Wavy Petal

Resources

Hats by Leko

www.hatsupply.com

Millinery supplies, stamens, ribbon, headbands, gelatin sizing

Jo-Ann Fabric and Craft Stores

www.joann.com

Nationwide locations

Judith M

www.judithm.com

Millinery supplies, gelatin sizing

Lacis

www.lacis.com

Flower irons, temperature controllers, flower iron tool heads

Michaels Arts & Crafts

www.michaels.com

Nationwide locations

Save-On-Crafts

www.save-on-crafts.com

Stamens, floral stem wire, ribbon

About the Author

You-Zhen Lu teaches fabric flower making in Taiwan. She is a certified lecturer for the Cut Ribbon Flower Association of Japan and is the founder of Youhong Fabric Flowers, a fabric flower making website.

Author Acknowledgements

I'd like to thank everyone at Elegant Books, as well as Sui Zhen and Sui Yun for all of their encouragement and guidance. Publishing this book has been a great experience.